MW00812778

Aroha Harris
(Ngā Puhi, Te Rarawa)

Aroha Harris is currently lecturing and completing doctoral research in history at the University of Auckland. She has considerable experience in both historical and social research, having worked for government agencies, private companies and iwi. Her current research interests are focussed on Māori in the twentieth century, especially since the end of World War Two.

Aroha has been published as a creative writer as well as an academic and researcher. Māori people are shaped by their history and whakapapa, and it is that sense of connectedness that Aroha tries to bring to her work.

HĪKOI

Forty Years of Māori Protest

Aroha Harris

First published in 2004 by
Huia Publishers, 39 Pipitea Street,
PO Box 17-335, Wellington,
Aotearoa New Zealand.
www.huia.co.nz

ISBN: 1-86969-101-6

Copyright © 2004 Aroha Harris

All rights reserved. No part of this publication may be reproduced,
stored in a retrieval system, or transmitted in any form or by any
means, electronic, mechanical, including photocopying, recording or
otherwise, without prior permission of the publisher.

National Library of New Zealand Cataloguing-in-Publication Data.

Harris, Aroha.
Hīkoi: forty years of Māori protest / Aroha Harris.
Includes bibliographical references.
ISBN 1-86969-101-6
1. Māori (New Zealand people)
2. Social action —New Zealand—History.
3. Protest movements—New Zealand—History.
4. New Zealand—Race relations—History. I. Title.
361.2308999442—dc 22

Cover image: Māori Land March 1975. Photograph by John Miller.

Printed in Thailand.

The support of Creative New Zealand is gratefully acknowledged.

ARTS COUNCIL OF NEW ZEALAND *TOI AOTEAROA*

Contents

He Kupu Whakatau, He Reo Mihi

Ehara taku toa i te toa takitahi, engari he toa takitini.

For me, this book is ingrained with memories of my nana who passed away unexpectedly, but peacefully, when I was in the throes of completing the draft manuscript. Nana – Violet Otene Harris, my paternal grandmother – was and is the person who anchored me in the world. She is a direct descendant of Poroa, the Te Rarawa tupuna represented by the pouwhenua that stands watch over the foreshore at Te Oneroa a Tohe. Poroa's daughter, Rihi, married Hohepa Otene Pura who was amongst those who signed the Treaty of Waitangi in 1840.

It is unsurprising that Nana was all about me as the book progressed, as she has been with so many of my projects throughout the years. One of the last things we did together was enjoy Hīkoi 2004 on its second day, when it paused briefly at Mangamuka before spending the night at Piki te Aroha Marae, Rāhiri. Nana was brimful of memories of the 1975 Land March passing through the same area almost three decades earlier. But she complained of a sore back, and was feeling the cold, so we did not stay too long – just long enough for her to dub the event Te Hīkoi Ātaahua.

Nana was more conservative than radical; she had sometimes participated in Waitangi Day celebrations, and never protested. But she was Māori – confidently and effortlessly: Ngāpuhi, Te Rarawa, whaea, wahine, kuia, dedicated to the marae and its community since her teenage years. She was her self, and in being herself she naturally supported many of the kaupapa included in the following pages. Te reo Māori was her first and best language, and in recent decades developments like kōhanga reo and Māori radio provided exciting new outlets for her to express it. Nana was very present to me, a steadying hand from an older quintessentially Māori world, and I dedicate this book, my first, to her wonderful memory. Nō reira, he mihi aroha, he roimata maumahara tēnei ki a koe, e Nana. E tangi tonu ana te ngākau.

The book began as an idea about three years ago, when Huia Publishers encouraged me to provide the text for a photographic history of modern Māori protest. The plan was to approach certain photographers to assist with images, and try to strike the right balance between text and photographs. The project developed slowly, spending generous periods on the back-burner. It was therefore amorphous and conceptual for a long time, largely inaccessible except by way of my imagination. Then the end came into view just as plans for Hīkoi 2004 were announced, so the project endured one last incarnation as the Hīkoi was woven into the manuscript.

This work has relied mainly on secondary sources, supplemented with newspaper research and a small amount of archival research. It could not have been written without the prior works of Dr Ranginui Walker, Māori history's most prolific writer, and the lofty mountain to whom this book bows.★ For every event included, there are many more omitted. There are clearly more stories, from a wide range of perspectives, yet to be written. However, some limitations were set by relative access to the images, and coverage of the sources. The book provides a broad narrative that acknowledges Māori protest as a modern phenomenon, while also remembering its descent from actions dating back to the nineteenth century. The whole is framed by the constancy of tino rangatiratanga as a political goal and partnered by splendid images of the times.

Many people contributed to this project, and I am indebted to them all. John Miller and Gil Hanly, two great chroniclers of New Zealand's modern protest history, kindly gave their time as their photographic collections were searched through. Tiopira McDowell, Tasha Jennings, Melissa Williams and Michael Tamihere – young, talented Māori university students and recent graduates – at various times, were the project's unassuming foot soldiers, all contributing in no small way to the research effort. Friends and whanaunga generously engaged in conversations that allowed me to quiz their memories, check facts and exchange ideas. I am especially grateful to Paparangi Reid, Haami Piripi, Hone Harawira, Cyril Chapman, and Paul Diamond; as well as Sharon Hawke and Te Miringa Hohaia who also offered valuable feedback and editing advice on draft material. Thanks are due to Robyn and Brian Bargh – whose patience and encouragement kept the project alive – and the rest of the team at Huia Publishers, particularly Heather Thom for her outstanding work researching images.

Heoi anō koutou mā, huri noa, huri noa, he mihi mahana, he mihi kau ana ki a koutou katoa i tautoko mai i tēnei mahi.

Aroha Harris
August 2004

★ A reference to the whakataukī : ki te tūohu koe, me he maunga teitei – if you bow your head, let it be to a lofty mountain.

Pouwhenua commemorating the Te Rarawa tupuna Poroa
- John Miller

Chapter One
The Rise and Rise of Māori Political Consciousness

ON 22 APRIL 2004, ANSWERING A CALL THAT HAD FIRST COME FROM Ngāti Kahungunu, hundreds of Māori and a small number of Pākehā gathered at Te Rerenga Wairua and began a long hīkoi south to Parliament. They were protesting against the Government's intention to eliminate Māori customary rights in the foreshore and seabed, an issue that had been percolating beneath the Māori–Crown relationship for many months beforehand. En route the core group of marchers was joined at different points by thousands of like-minded New Zealand citizens of all ages and ethnic, religious and political backgrounds. Finally on 5 May – two weeks and 11,000 kilometres later – the various strands of the hīkoi, which had come from all parts of the country, converged in Wellington and an estimated gathering of 25,000 people marched on Parliament. Hīkoi 2004 became a spectacular display of Māori transcending tribal difference to express their shared dissatisfaction with government policy.

If not repeating itself, history had certainly come full circle. For the second time in thirty years Māori had united under the rallying cry of land loss. Cyril Chapman handed the carved pouwhenua that was to be carried at the fore of the Hīkoi to its first bearer. Symbolic of land loss, Chapman had carried it himself in 1975 as a young man on the Māori Land March. A lot has happened since Whina Cooper took the first steps of the Land March. Hīkoi 2004 now provides a useful landmark against which modern Māori protest can be viewed, and this book attempts a visual statement of some of Māori protest's key campaigns. Many things have changed significantly since the advent of modern Māori activism. But clearly – as expressed in the sadness people felt at having to embark on such a protest in the twenty-first century – some things have remained the same.

Te Oneroa a Tohe (Ninety Mile Beach) on the first day of Hīkoi 2004 - *Northern Advocate*

Māori Leadership Conference, Taumarunui 1963 - Ans Westra

Modern Māori protest is often seen as the exuberant and youthful rebel to the comparatively conservative leadership of organisations like the Māori Women's Welfare League and New Zealand Māori Council. Both the league and the Maori council were known for their support of the leadership of young men and women.

Ans Westra   Ans Westra   Ans Westra

The images reproduced in the pages that follow make great photographic history. It is clear from the images that Māori protest is not the disorganised and isolated activity of a minority radical element, the view so often portrayed by politicians, commentators and the media. Modern Māori activism, with its roots firmly planted in the history of contesting and negotiating the treaty relationship between Māori and the Crown, has been a strong and consistent feature of Māori society in the second half of the twentieth century. Throughout, the politics of rangatiratanga have been constant, embracing both positive action towards a shared goal, and active resistance to State goals that emphasised assimilation which many Māori viewed as detrimental to the long-term life of Māori society and culture.

The era of modern Māori protest began in the late 1960s. Precipitated by a number of events and trends which highlighted incidents of racism and an ongoing failure on the Government's part to understand Māori aspirations, it experienced its heyday in the 1970s and 1980s. But if protest is about disputing, objecting, contesting and remonstrating, then it is a long-established characteristic of Māori interaction with Pākehā and with the State, spanning practically two centuries. The cornerstones of Māori protest – land, the Treaty of Waitangi, te reo, mana Māori motuhake and tino rangatiratanga – have stood firmly throughout history and the Māori experience of colonisation. Even the activities that usually distinguish modern protest from earlier forms – pickets, demonstrations, occupations, hīkoi – can also be found in the nineteenth century. There are, for example, nineteenth-century precedents for occupations like those at Raglan and Bastion Point in the 1970s, and Pākaitore in the 1990s. In 1877 about 100 people, under the leadership of Te Maiharoa, occupied a sheep station at Ōmārama to draw attention to the outstanding land claims of Ngāi Tahu. A lesser-known occupation occurred around the turn of the twentieth century at Mangapehi when local Māori pitched a tent across the railway track during a dispute with a local timber milling company. Similarly, civil disobedience has featured at many Waitangi Day protests since the 1970s, as well as in the non-violent resistance protests of Te Whiti o Rongomai and Tohu Kakahi at Parihaka 100 years earlier.

Māori Women's Welfare League Garden Party in 1962 and Rotorua conference 1963 - Ans Westra

Ans Westra

Ans Westra

Ans Westra

While modern Māori protest may be traced down its own rich, indigenous historical lines it may also be discerned in its own context and space and time. It arrived on the tail of the quiescent fifties; the exuberant and youthful rebel to the comparatively conservative leadership of state-sponsored organisations like the Māori Women's Welfare League and New Zealand Māori Council. It was also part of a protest family that emerged in the 1960s and matured in the seventies and eighties into rights movements organised around tangata whenua, women and gays. The Prime Minister Keith Holyoake announced New Zealand's participation in the Vietnam War in 1965, and quickly provoked an anti-war campaign that lasted till 1972. The developing dissenting mood was broadcast to the nation through the recently intro-duced medium of television. Laden with the Vietnam War, television news covered both international and local protest. In the 1960s, opposition to sporting contacts with South Africa grew in intensity, and some young Māori developed a political affinity with the civil rights movement in the United States, including revolutionary liberation movements like the Black Panther Party.

These broader trends and influences played some role in shaping the nature and style of Māori activism. But it was the policies of the New Zealand Government – especially those that continued the perennial push for assimilation – which provided a more immediate, home-grown catalyst for the rising voice of Māori discontent. Assimilation, and later integration, sought to socialise Māori into the modern urbanised world and the social and economic life of the nation. While arguably an innocent and even desirable goal, in practice it seemed to require Māori to forsake their identity and did little if anything to support the integrity of Māori society. Rapid assimilation threatened to destroy Māori culture. Within that policy framework, Māori interaction with the State following World War Two, proceeded on a relatively even keel through a bureaucracy, the Department of Māori Affairs, which was prepared to include and work with Māori community leadership. Indeed, the Māori Social and Economic Advancement Act 1945 deliberately drew the network of tribal committees established during the war into the operation of the department's Welfare Division. The department also supported the Māori Women's Welfare League, formally constituted in 1951. The tribal committees, branches of the league and the department's team of Māori welfare officers worked together on projects of mutual interest. And later, in 1962, the Māori council became the national organisation representing tribal and district Māori committees, and a permanent consultative body through which Māori leadership and the Government could communicate.

Despite the appearance of friendly cooperation a level of suspicion, especially of the Department of Māori Affairs, simmered under the surface even during the best times.

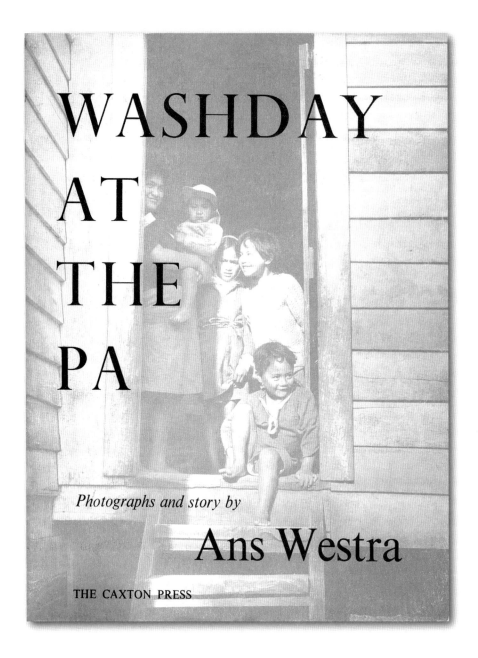

Although New Zealand had an international reputation for harmonious race relations, incidents of petty racism against Māori were known to occur. By the middle of the 1960s one of the country's most treasured myths was being increasingly scrutinised and critiqued.

Reaction to the department's relocation programme provides a useful example. The programme began in 1961 and aimed to assist Māori who were shifting from rural to urban areas. The programme has been rightly criticised for its role in the process of urbanising Māori. But it was hardly used compared to the thousands of Māori who were urbanising. In its first year of operation, the Taitokerau region complained that no one had used the programme, and in its second year only a small number. Despite the many factors that influenced urbanisation, there were Māori who could not be encouraged to forsake what were perceived as their emotional attachments to ancestral land and move closer to centres of employment, even with the inducement of easy-to-get mortgages.[1]

There were other times when protest and resistance could be found interspersed amongst the activities of a relatively collaborative and conservative Māori leadership. The welfare league accepted the department's considerable material and financial support, as well as the participation and influence of the female welfare officers. But it also embarked on an ambitious housing survey, consequently calling into question the department's housing programme and lobbying for representation on regional housing priority committees. It began questioning government policy on Māori language in schools almost immediately it was established, and in 1964 led public criticism of a Department of Education publication, *Washday at the Pa. Washday* contained a series of photos linked by a simple narrative to depict a day in the life of a rural Māori family. The league's strong and adverse critique claimed that distribution of the booklet to schools had led to Māori children being taunted by their peers. It was stereotypical rather than typical, and did nothing to foster positive images of Māori. Significantly, the league also asserted that the department ought to have consulted with either the league or the Māori council before going to print.

While continuing to negotiate the Māori–State relationship, Māori also dealt with the ongoing petty racism of Pākehā fellow-citizens. Although largely unreported, the kind of racism that restricted Māori access to restaurants, hotels, cinemas, barbers and accommodation was a feature of Māori experience in the twentieth century, especially during the post-war years as an urbanising Māori population lived and worked more and more under the gaze of the Pākehā. Furthermore, anthropology of the time revealed that Pākehā attitudes to Māori set up stereotypes which said that Pākehā were healthier, better educated, less criminal, in higher status jobs, wealthier and living in better conditions. Māori on the other hand were musical, lazy, happy-go-lucky, physically strong, failures, unattractive, and generous. Happy-go-lucky and generous were not necessarily compliments: being happy-go-lucky was regarded as a dysfunctional trait within a modern society that demanded modern work ethics. Similarly, Māori were seen as generous to a fault, to the point of foolishly causing their

Protests against Vietnam War, Wellington 1972 - *Dominion Post Collection, Alexander Turnbull Library*

Protests against Vietnam War, Wellington 1972 - *Dominion Post Collection, Alexander Turnbull Library*

The development of Māori protest dovetailed with trends in local and international protest movements of the 1960s and 1970s, including civil rights movements in the United States and opposition to the war in Vietnam.

own improvidence. Such stereotypes were further perpetuated by a New Zealand press that distorted the picture of Māori affairs and contributed to misunderstandings between Māori and Pākehā.[2]

Even so, racism was largely something that Māori experienced in the margins of society, and it was rarely explicitly exposed in public. One exception occurred early in 1959 when Dr Henry Bennett was refused service at the lounge bar of the Papakura Hotel: the publican had imposed a 'colour bar' because his Pākehā patrons objected to the behaviour of his Māori ones. The hotel dealt with the incident swiftly and the specific incident spent a very short time in the public spotlight, which can partly be attributed to the magnanimity of Bennett himself. But reporting of the incident did uncover other specific examples of racial discrimination in the area. Another Papakura hotel imposed a similar restriction against Māori. The Pukekohe Hotel banned Māori women from the European women's lounge, and Māori in the

Pukekohe district were restricted to the cheapest seats in the local cinema, except for a quota of twenty-eight. In the onslaught of letters to editors that followed, two main camps could be perceived: Pākehā who were surprised that such discrimination could happen in New Zealand, and concerned about protecting the country's reputation for harmonious race relations; and Māori who were exasperated that Pākehā were so oblivious to the reality of racial discrimination in society. A smaller group rationalised the use of colour bars saying that they were minor, existed for good reasons (usually reasons of hygiene), and were thankfully far less harsh than those in other countries. Apparently society could tolerate a modicum of racism, provided New Zealand never lost its standing as the country with the best race relations in the world.[3]

Five years after the Bennett incident, New Zealand's wholesome and rosy picture of racial harmony was repainted by the league's critique of *Washday at the Pa*. The booklet was withdrawn from schools and destroyed. But the Pākehā public and the press came out primarily in favour of the book and opposed to its withdrawal. A second edition was published in November 1964, albeit privately and with an accompanying publisher's note summarising the public outcry that had followed, and quoting extensively from the press. Whereas the public response to the Bennett incident was relatively contained, the response to *Washday* was unprecedented and widespread, played out across the land in editorials, letters to editors, student newspapers, and the newsletters of various organisations. Statements from the New Zealand Educational Institute, the Māori council, MP for Southern Māori Sir Eruera Tirikatene, the booklet's photographer Ans Westra, the league, the Minister of Education, and even James K. Baxter were published. The only point that the general public was willing to concede, was that the title was misleading because the book was not set in a pā. But it was also argued that using the term 'pā' constituted a gross mistake because for Pākehā it was a term loaded with the negative connotations of poverty, primitive conditions, and material and moral bankruptcy.[4]

The commentaries surrounding the Bennett and *Washday* incidents combined to expose the usually discreet underbelly of New Zealand's race relations. Beneath the veneer of a persistently idealised picture was a very unhappy situation. Academic studies allowed academics to talk to each other about race. But the wider public did not, as a general rule, participate in the discourse. Mostly Pākehā New Zealand continued on unaware of its own racism, until these seemingly isolated, although not unnoticed, controversies were held up to public scrutiny. The Government conceded there were some occasional problems; but content that no legislation allowed for racial discrimination, it made no attempt to outlaw or even monitor it. Instead, Pākehā racism was expected to subside naturally as Māori became more and more assimilated. By the middle of the 1960s cracks were visible in one of the country's most treasured myths. Soon after, the sledgehammer of modern activism was poised to descend.

While battling overt racism on one front, Māori society could also be found on another warding off the detrimental effects of government policies anxious to complete the assimilation programme first laid out in the nineteenth century. Assimilation took on the modern guise of 'integration', and was pursued with new fervour following the publication in 1961 of J. K. Hunn's *Report on the Department of Māori Affairs,* popularly referred to as the Hunn Report. The report attempted to address the new challenges facing a Māori population that had rapidly transformed from small, isolated, tribal and rural to large, pan-tribal and urban. The trauma of this social upheaval was further highlighted by the report's comprehensive statistical analysis, which presented a grim picture of Māori disadvantage in health, education, employment, crime, housing, and land development. Yet the solutions the Hunn Report proposed were perhaps more disconcerting than the problems it revealed.

Ultimately, if successfully pursued, integration would reduce the Department of Māori Affairs to a small coordinating agency with a watching brief over other departments, to which Māori Affairs' existing functions would gradually be mainstreamed. Māori people would be socially engineered into effective citizens, fully participating in the social, political and economic life of the nation in modern ways that aligned them with their Pākehā counterparts. In effect, Māori families and communities – that had until then entered into relationships with the Department of Māori Affairs – would gradually be abandoned and left to departments that had neither the experience nor necessarily the inclination, to work with them in the same way Māori Affairs had. The natural forces of integration – such as intermarriage, modern housing, public schools, inter-racial contact in the workplace and suburbs – were to be acknowledged and embraced and, where possible, promoted by official policy. 'Pepper-potting', for example, not only located Māori families in predominantly Pākehā communities but could also be quite effective at preventing groups of related families from settling in the same suburb. Segregation, like that perceived in the Māori secondary schools, tribalism and sentimental attachments to land were all targeted as factors impeding the Māori path to integration and therefore good race relations. The definition of what constituted Māori also caught Hunn's attention. He suggested that the numerous definitions in place ought to be reconciled and tightened to restrict the numbers of Māori entitled to the 'privileges of special legislation'.

Hunn's one concession to Māori aspirations was the idea that the integration of Māori people should not preclude the preservation of Māori culture; Māori would become New Zealanders with distinct cultural (but not social or political) characteristics. Hunn's definition of Māori culture was narrow and naive: 'haka and poi' and 'arts and crafts'. But he wanted the bedrocks of Māori tribal and individual identity, like tūrangawaewae, to happily submit to modern western equivalents, like the quarter-acre section. Furthermore, those aspects of Māori culture that could be

Waitangi Day protest, Wellington 1986 - Gil Hanly

In the 1980s protests concerning government
responsibilities to Māori were being held
throughout the country.

retained would have to be saved from the brink of death by Māori people's own limited resources and from a position of severe social and economic disadvantage. It seems the onus for integration was on Māori. Māori were expected to fit into Pākehā society in the interests of race relations, but nothing encouraged Pākehā to develop even a small level of understanding of the Māori world. The notion that the State could assist such a process, or actively support the preservation of Māori culture, was not even considered.

For Māori then, and their handful of Pākehā supporters, integration was merely assimilation by another name, and assimilation had been practised informally long before Hunn's report made it official. For much of the twentieth century, Māori land legislation had focussed on reforming Māori land titles to something less communal and more cognisant with the individual ownership that Pākehā society preferred. One such ploy was the compulsory alienation of 'uneconomic' Māori land interests introduced by the Māori Affairs Act 1953, which caused considerable resentment amongst Māori including the Māori members of Parliament. In welfare, Māori adoptions had long been handled by the Māori Land Court pretty much along traditional lines, but in 1955 they were drawn into the same legislative framework as adoptions generally. That same year, the mainstreaming of native schools began. These schools had become integral to Māori communities all over the country for reasons beyond the education they provided, but their integration in the mainstream was boosted following the Hunn Report, and concluded in 1969. Post-Hunn the attention of Māori policy turned squarely to the cities, where integration was most required. Under the new regime, it was up to individuals to choose to maintain their whānau, hapū, and iwi links, whereas previous generations of Māori welfare officers and Māori leaders had stressed the general importance of tribal organisation and worked within that frame.

Although opposition to the Hunn Report was extensive, the Minister of Māori Affairs, Ralph Hanan, encouraged its progression to the implementation phase. However, when attempts were made to implement Hunn's recommendations for Māori land titles, they met with a concerted Māori opposition that also ushered in the new vanguard of Māori protest. Hunn's focus for Māori land had been on reducing multiple-ownership by compulsorily acquiring Māori land interests, restricting succession, and increasing the value of the already controversial uneconomic shares. When even the usually agreeable Māori council failed to support the proposals the Government tried to by-pass Māori cooperation by commissioning an independent report from Ivor Prichard and Hone Waetford. Prichard was a former chief judge of the Māori Land Court, and Waetford an interpreter. Their report into the system of Māori land titles, submitted in late 1965, basically reinforced Hunn's recommenda-

Waitangi Day protest, Auckland 1989 - Gil Hanly

tions. The Government followed through by introducing and passing the widely vaunted Māori Affairs Amendment Act 1967. The act introduced provisions to compulsorily change the status of land held by four or fewer owners from Māori to 'European'. It allowed for greater intervention in Māori land administration by the Department of Māori Affairs and Māori Trustee, provided for the free-holding of Māori reserved and vested lands, and increased the value of uneconomic shares.

Māori opposition was vehement. The pockets of dissatisfaction and criticism that government officials seemed used to blossomed into organised and widespread resistance. Admonishment came from all quarters – national, regional and local organisations, Māori individuals and groups, both urban and rural – and maintained a grave watch over the Prichard–Waetford Report, the bill and finally the passage of the 1967 act . Quickly dubbed the 'last land grab', Māori viewed the act as the Crown's final attack on the remnants of their tribal property, and responded with a major and cohesive Māori land rights movement that led directly to the 1975 Māori Land March.

Amongst the many critics was a group of Māori university students and graduates, which evolved a few years later into Ngā Tamatoa. Members were young, educated, and urbanised; some were unionists, others experienced political activists. They

Waitangi Day protest, Wellington 1987 - Gil Hanly

were leaders and social commentators recently come-of-age, the new face of Māori activism. For Ngā Tamatoa, Māori affairs policy provided some immediate catalysts for modern Māori protest. Although many of the issues they raised were long-standing, like te reo and the Treaty of Waitangi, the reasons for protest and resistance were contemporary, like the politics of integration and marginalisation in the cities. Ngā Tamatoa also heralded a new analysis of the Māori experience of colonisation; one that understood racism and how it worked.

Ngā Tamatoa did not so much replace the old guard, the leadership of the 1950s and 1960s, but rather challenged it to face new choices and strategies for articulating Māori grievances and engaging with the State. The things that distinguished the modern activists from the conservatives of old were more a matter of means than ends: the goals and aspirations of Māori development have long been shared across the spectrum of Māori politics. The Māori council and the league continued their typical kinds of remonstration – letter-writing, petitions, remits, deputations to relevant ministers of Parliament or government officials, and published public statements. But the young activists were inclined to choose more spirited and forceful actions like marches, pickets, demonstrations and occupations. For the activists, civil disobedience was an option even at the risk of arrest, and although they consistently enjoyed some support from the conservative quarters of their kuia and kaumātua, the fact they also faced the scorn and derision of their own people cannot be overlooked.

Ngā Tamatoa was the progenitor of a Māori movement that would eventually comprise a potent collection of Māori protest groups and individuals: politically conscious, radical, and unwaveringly committed to the pursuit of tino rangatiratanga. This movement lent its weight to a smorgasbord of causes and campaigns. And the decades following its emergence have been punctuated by some of the main events of Aotearoa's protest history: numerous Waitangi Day actions including the 1984 Hīkoi ki Waitangi; the 1975 Land March; the occupations of Bastion Point, Raglan and Pākaitore; the first Māori Language Day; He Taua; the 1981 Springbok Tour demonstrations; and widespread rejection of the fiscal envelope 1994–95. A cynic might view these and numerous other related actions as an inchoate scattering of radical discontent. But they were all bound by a rising Māori political consciousness centred on a set of recurring themes, and supported by a kind of underground education. Workshops, hui, newsletters – and, more recently, websites and email groups – have all contributed. The movement's consciousness raising and assertiveness training, structural analysis and decolonisation workshops have generated a genuine cultural solidarity amongst Māori.

The past was often invoked as a source of inspiration and a reminder that modern activism was just another incarnation in a long line of indigenous movements designed to recover and reassert tino rangatiratanga and tribal authority, which the Crown had wrested from Māori despite the promises of the Treaty of Waitangi. Slogans that cried 'Get off Māori Land' and 'The Treaty is a Fraud' sat alongside the historical quest for mana Māori motuhake. The teachings of nineteenth-century visionaries like Te Whiti o Rongomai and Te Kooti Arikirangi Te Turuki; the bold twentieth-century aspiration of Tahupotiki Wiremu Ratana to have the treaty ratified in law; the political vitality of the Kotahitanga movement, the Kīngitanga and the Young Māori Party all provided the historical lines down which modern activism could trace its origins. Land was a prism through which Māori could see their loss of culture and identity refracted. Te reo Māori became another of the motifs of Māori activism, and in the early seventies a campaign led by Ngā Tamatoa and the Wellington-based Te Reo Māori Society pushed for te reo to be taught in schools, and established a Māori Language Day. Subsequent achievements have included kōhanga reo, kura kaupapa Māori, whare wānanga and Māori print and broadcast media. However, whatever the kaupapa, there is no escaping the constancy of the Treaty of Waitangi as a focal point for Māori protest. Protest essentially retrieved the treaty from the

MOOHR banner at Parliament 1970 - John Miller

dustbin of history, and reminded the nation that it contained promises to Māori that Māori took very seriously.

Māori treaty consciousness had continued and developed unbroken since its signing in 1840. The treaty has been the cornerstone of Māori struggles to secure the rights that it guarantees, regain control of Māori affairs, and have their tangata whenua status recognised. By contrast, the Pākehā consciousness of the treaty that developed in the 1960s was an offshoot of their concerns for nationhood, citizenship and the 'one people' philosophy. Implementing the treaty's guarantees was not in their frame. By 1971 annual Waitangi Day celebrations had reduced the treaty to a somewhat flaccid symbol of nationhood. Ngā Tamatoa drew attention to the Māori reality, a cultural divide that marginalised Māori. In 1973 it declared Waitangi Day a day to mourn the loss of Māori land, and its members wore black armbands to the celebrations. When the Government turned to the Māori council for support in chastising the protestors, the council responded by producing a submission citing fourteen statutes that were in breach of the treaty.

Effectively it was the Māori activism of the seventies that left a wake in which successive governments could slowly think about giving the treaty greater recognition, and the Waitangi Tribunal could begin its work. With Matiu Rata as Minister of Māori Affairs, the Treaty of Waitangi Act 1975 established the Waitangi Tribunal as an independent commission of inquiry tasked with investigating and making recommendations about claims relating to breaches of the treaty. Rata was also responsible for the Māori Affairs Amendment Act 1974 which attempted to undo the 'invasion of rights' inherent in the 1967 act.[5] But it was too little, too late. These and other government actions in the 1970s were insufficient to quell Māori protest. Waitangi Day became an annual focus of protest activity which challenged the Government to honour the treaty in practical terms if it wanted to celebrate its signing.

For its first ten years little public attention was granted the Waitangi Tribunal. It could only consider claims that had occurred since its establishment until, in 1985, it was empowered to consider claims retrospectively to 1840. Consequently the tribunal was inundated with claims as iwi vied to have the tribally specific injustices of the past acknowledged and then compensated for. But the business of articulating, negotiating and settling long-standing iwi resource claims is a painstakingly slow process that has largely captured Māori energies for nearly twenty years. Anecdotal evidence suggests that for Māori the process is more battle than arbitration – a courtroom and boardroom battle, but a battle nonetheless. Despite their flaws, the treaty claims process coupled with the Government's devolution policies of the eighties have sometimes been credited with contributing to the revitalisation of iwi organisation and activity experienced throughout much of Aotearoa. While Māori attention was diverted, Māori activism was believed to have taken a well-earned break. If laid out on a continuum a decline in the intensity and frequency of radical Māori activism can be detected in the late 1980s. But it was short-lived. In 1994 and 1995, Māori overwhelmingly rejected and protested against the Bolger government's 'fiscal envelope', which capped government spending on all historical treaty claims at one billion dollars, and excluded Department of Conservation lands from any settlement packages. About the same time the Māori rights group, Te Ahi Kaa, led an eighty-day occupation of Pākaitore by Whanganui Māori – an action that received considerable public criticism, but also much support from Māori and Pākehā around the country. Protest activity settled into another relatively quiet period from the late 1990s. But Hīkoi 2004 – a gentle giant uncharacteristically devoid of arrests – came as a massive reminder of the ability of Māori activism to mobilise the people around kaupapa that are genuinely shared by the masses.

There was a surreal aspect to the events that surrounded and preceded the Hīkoi. It was as if the first part of 2004 had been cast into a perpetual state of déjà vu, as history visited both sides of the House. In January, the Leader of the Opposition Don Brash delivered his infamous Orewa speech. Sounding remarkably like a disciple of Hunn's integration, Brash advocated 'one rule for all' and an end to racial divisiveness. It was a speech that even his own spokesperson on Māori Affairs, Georgina Te Heuheu, could not bring herself to support preferring instead to relinquish her portfolio. Yet Brash, and his new spokesperson Gerry Brownlee, continued with the political rhetoric of a bygone era. Meanwhile, Māori and the Labour government grappled with the issues surrounding ownership of the takutaimoana, or foreshore and seabed. Labour proposed to rescind the right of Māori to have the nature and extent of their customary interests in the takutaimoana investigated by the Māori Land Court. Instead it would assume ownership itself on behalf of the Crown and the public. Māori concerns were expected to be placated by provision for the court to recognise their ancestral connections to discrete stretches of coastline. Past and present warped, as the last land grab of 1967 prepared for relegation to second-to-last, and banners and badges insisted 'No Raupatu in Our Time'.

Māori opposition to the Government's proposals had been made clear over a period of months. Te Ope Mana a Tai, an iwi-based collective set up in July 2003, gave the kaupapa the requisite leadership by facilitating discussion and debate and disseminating information and guidance. In February 2004, Te Rarawa hosted 'Hands Across the Beach' at Ahipara, in which some two thousand people participated in a symbolic hand-holding ceremony that peacefully demonstrated the manawhenua relationship of iwi and their land, and their role as kaitiaki. Then in March Ngāti Kahungunu announced that they would hīkoi to Wellington with a view to arriving around the time that the Foreshore and Seabed Bill was due to come before Parliament. Hīkoi 2004 grew, very quickly, from there. It was a compelling reminder of both the achievements of earlier protest actions, and the knottier problems of Māori–Pākehā relations yet to be resolved.

As it made its way through the country the Hīkoi had to contend with the backlash unleashed by Brash's Orewa speech and subsequent posturing. In Auckland two-fingered salutes, talkback radio vitriol and obscenities shouted from moving vehicles were directed at those on the Hīkoi, including the very young and the very old, and regardless of their race, creed or political suasion. Prime Minister Helen Clark lashed out by announcing she preferred the company of a celebrity sheep to that of Hīkoi participants, who were, according to her, being led by a selection of 'haters and wreckers'.

Rather incongruously, Māori seemed quietly self-assured. The fruits of forty years of modern activism rallied around. Coverage of the Hīkoi was carried – often live – by Māori broadcast and print media. The Māori magazine *Tū Mai* hosted an online petition, and the Hīkoi and the issues it bore could be found nightly on Māori news delivered in te reo Māori by the Māori Television Service. Māori TV was only a few weeks old when the Hīkoi left Te Rerenga Wairua, and although a success its launch had been marred by Brash's continued panning of what he considered separatist, tax-wasting misadventures. Yet the fact that Māori media were robust enough to provide such comprehensive

coverage was a tribute to Māori education and language initiatives, the seeds for which had been planted by an earlier wave of activism. Unfortunately, the same sense of achievement could not be taken from the fact that Māori representation in Parliament, numerically at least, had never been greater. And probably no one who marched in 1975 under the slogan 'not one more acre [of land]' could have predicted that a twenty-first-century government could engender despair and exasperation of such magnitude that Māori would so resolutely answer the call to march again. At least one lesson of Hīkoi 2004 is clear: rather than never repeating, history is fated to repeat, and repeat again, until its lessons are learned.

Hīkoi 2004 in Wellington - Clayton Tume

Chapter Two

Rugby, Racism and Human Rights

LOOKING BACK, PROTEST APPEARS ENDEMIC TO THE 1960S. Actions opposing the war in Vietnam received considerable public attention, and opposition to sporting contacts with South Africa began to develop a momentum that would famously climax in 1981. In New Zealand, these and other movements were interlaced with an emerging Māori activism that would stress Māori rights and malign the racism that Māori faced in society.

By 1960 rugby was well-established as New Zealand's national game, and Māori featured amongst its greatest players and supporters. Rugby ought to have been one of the forces of integration that J. K. Hunn so wanted Māori to embrace. But in the face of mounting disagreement the New Zealand Rugby Football Union (NZRFU) continued to send racially selected teams to play in South Africa. The NZRFU's position invited the 'No Maoris, No Tour' campaign against the 1960 All Black tour of South Africa, from which Māori were refused selection. While significant, the campaign did not win the support of Prime Minister Walter Nash who chose not to intervene. A later tour, scheduled for 1967, was cancelled because Māori were to be excluded once again. In 1970 Māori were selected to play South Africa for the first time, but as honorary whites. It seemed a reasonable compromise for most rugby-lovers, but it did nothing to subdue growing anti-apartheid protest.

Māori involved in these early protests developed their own flax-roots analysis of the situation. A petition headed by Anglican Bishop Wiremu Netana Panapa began with a reminder that the Treaty of Waitangi promised equality between Māori and Pākehā. It also framed the exclusion of Māori from the 1960 tour in terms of the numerous acts of discrimination that Māori experienced at the hands of publicans,

Myers Park, Auckland 1960 - *Auckland Art Gallery Toi o Tamaki, gift of Marti Friedlander, with assistance from the Elise Mourant bequest*

All Black trial, Wellington 1970 - John Miller

By 1960 rugby was well-established as New Zealand's national game, and Māori featured amongst its greatest players and supporters. In the face of mounting disagreement the New Zealand Rugby Football Union (NZRFU) continued to send racially selected teams to play in South Africa.

Demonstrations against Springbok tour, Wellington 1970 - Ans Westra

barbers and cinema owners, although the NZRFU was charged with committing 'the most flagrant, single act of racial discrimination ever to have taken place in New Zealand'.[6] The petition could have requested a simple intervention from government on the particular matter of sporting contacts with South Africa. Instead, it lifted the matter from the rugby field and settled it into the quagmire that was New Zealand's race relationship. The petition proposed that the Government issue a formal policy statement on race relations and racial equality, and one that could monitor discriminatory practices. By the end of the sixties no such policy was forthcoming, and the debate surrounding apartheid and sporting contacts was no closer to being resolved. Some Māori seemed appeased by the decision to send Māori players as honorary whites on the 1970 tour, but not the Māori Women's Welfare League. Breaking ranks with its brother organisation the New Zealand Māori Council, which had come out in support of the 1970 tour, the league advised the NZRFU of its opposition. Conferring the title 'honorary white' on Māori All Blacks was an 'insult to the Māori race' and opposing the tour let the world know that the league opposed the policy of apartheid.[7]

In 1968, within a year of the amendment to the Māori Affairs Act passing into legislation and amidst the sea of growing political awareness, two newsletters appeared on the Wellington streets, *Te Hokioi* and *MOOHR* (Māori Organisation on Human Rights). *Te Hokioi* took its name from the Kīngitanga newspaper first published in 1861, at a time that the Government was at war with Māori in Taranaki and Waikato.

Both *Te Hokioi* and *MOOHR* were closely associated with Pākehā protest groups. Each had some involvement with the class struggle of trade unions and the anti-apartheid campaign, and relationships with those willing to ally themselves with the Māori cause were actively cultivated. *MOOHR* aimed to defend the rights of Māori and other minority groups by drawing on the rights and provisions set out in the

Marti Friedlander Archive, on loan from the artist to Auckland Art Gallery Toi o Tamaki

Dennis Brutus, a leading South African anti-apartheid campaigner
being welcomed to New Zealand in 1969 by Syd Jackson,
Nga Tamatoa.

In 1970 Māori were selected to play South Africa
for the first time, but as honorary whites.
It seemed a reasonable compromise for most
rugby-lovers, but it did nothing to subdue
growing anti-apartheid protest.

Dominion Post Collection, Alexander Turnbull Library

Parliamentarians joined the protest against the jailing of the Dean
of Johannesburg in 1971 for anti-apartheid activity.

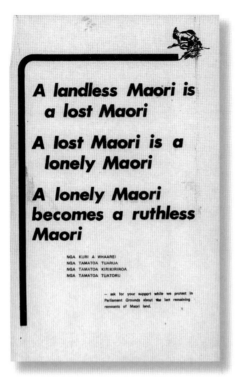

A landless Maori is
a lost Maori

A lost Maori is a
lonely Maori

A lonely Maori
becomes a ruthless
Maori

NGA KURI A WHAAREI
NGA TAMATOA TUARUA
NGA TAMATOA KIRIKIRIROA
NGA TAMATOA TUATORU

— ask for your support while we protest in
Parliament Grounds about the last remaining
remnants of Maori land.

Peter Franks Collection, Alexander Turnbull Library

Trevor Richards Collection,
Alexander Turnbull Library

Treaty of Waitangi and the United Nation's Universal Declaration of Human Rights. *Te Hokioi* proclaimed itself 'a taiaha for truth', and provided a radical Māori perspective on the problems its writings exposed. Both newsletters opposed apartheid, racism in all spheres of social and political life, and Māori involvement in unjust wars overseas. Their goals included raising Māori political consciousness, as well as public awareness of Māori rights and the ways in which government legislation eroded them.

In print, these goals translated into articles that exposed environmental concerns for pollution and the exploitation of kaimoana and other natural resources, the struggles of Māori fighting to retain their lands, and New Zealand's military involvement in wars in Malaysia and Vietnam. Human rights featured prominently, including the anti-apartheid movement led by Halt All Racist Tours (HART) and Citizens Association for Racial Equality (CARE), the work of the United Nations, and overseas struggles against colonisation, racism and the exploitation of workers. Land loss was a dominant theme in *Te Hokioi*. It publicised and supported individual Māori land claims, and printed lists of unclaimed Māori monies and land interests. In its articles on the prevalence of racial discrimination, *MOOHR* took particular interest in the justice system. It discussed police harassment of protestors, Māori youth and gang

Demonstrations against Springbok tour, Wellington 1970 - John Miller

The Māori Organisation on Human Rights (MOOHR) aimed to defend the rights of Māori and other minority groups by drawing on the rights and provisions set out in the Treaty of Waitangi and the United Nation's Universal Declaration of Human Rights.

Protestors at Parliament 1972 - John Miller

members. It described some of the negative experiences of young Māori offenders subjected to the justice system, and advised Māori on their legal rights when dealing with the police and appearing before the court. Later Ngā Tamatoa would actively involve itself with the difficulties facing Māori youth in the justice system, defending young Māori from police discrimination, and accessing legal aid for them.

Although *Te Hokioi* and *MOOHR* had a very wide support and interest base they were essentially Māori in motivation, analysis and scope. They drew also on the philosophies of Marxism and white liberalism, the ruminations of academics, and the analyses of the civil rights and anti-apartheid movements. But they remained deeply aware of their place in Māori history. Each of them was established as a direct response to the 1967 act, and parallels were drawn between that act and confiscation legislation of the 1860s. They took heed of the words and deeds of their ancestors, and emphasised the importance of Māori identity, culture and language. They also articulated Māori views in new and embryonic ways, historicising contemporary issues and foretelling the new wave of Māori activism.

Ngā Tamatoa at Parliament 1972 - John Miller

Ngā Tamatoa, Waiomio 1972 - John Miller

Ngā Tamatoa was the progenitor of a Māori movement that would eventually comprise a potent collection of Māori protest groups and individuals; politically conscious, radical, and unwaveringly committed to the pursuit of tino rangatiratanga.

John Miller

In 1972 Tame Iti and others set up a tent as a 'Māori Embassy' on the lawn at Parliament as an assertion of tino rangatiratanga. His arrest and subsequent dismissal of charges continued to focus attention on Māori grievances.

John Miller

Dominion Post

Chapter Three
Our Language is Our Culture

Ko te reo te mauri o te mana Māori

ONE OF THE MOST LONG-STANDING MOTIFS OF MĀORI ACTIVISM is the loss of culture is epitomised by the language, te reo. During the first part of the twentieth century Apirana Ngata had been a staunch advocate of ensuring all aspects of Māori culture survived modernisation, including tribal (political) organisation. He promoted the active use of te reo at home and in the community, while also seeing an important place for English-language education. From the 1950s the Māori Women's Welfare League had begun questioning government policy on the teaching of te reo and Māori history in schools, and later some of its members had limited success promoting the idea of Māori playcentres. But these early advocates had to pitch themselves against schools that actively prohibited the reo in their grounds. And 1960 it was clear that policies of integration meant that Māori would be influenced to make English their first language. In the words of Hunn, te reo was a relic of an ancient life that would be difficult to keep alive. In addition, as the Waitangi Tribunal would later hear, schools, the media, government departments and the courts were monocultural and monolingual. Even if they would deign to welcome the Māori language, they were ill-equipped to receive it. Opportunities to hear and speak Māori publicly were severely restricted, and government indifference meant the public and officialdom held it in low esteem.

Concern for the ailing state of Māori language and culture was picked up again in earnest in 1970, when the Māori council convened a Young Māori Leaders' Conference at the University of Auckland. The conference, an annual fixture on the Māori calendar, brought together kuia and kaumātua, members of the Māori council and the welfare league, Māori incorporations, trust boards, unions, students, gang members and church leaders.[8] The 1970 conference produced a report for submission to the Government. Amongst its many concerns were the preservation of te reo me ōna tikanga, and fostering understanding and respect for Māori and Māori culture among Pākehā. Conference participants voiced their anger and frustration

Archives New Zealand/Te Rua Mahara o te Kāwanatanga

One of the most long-standing motifs of Māori
activism is the loss of culture, epitomised by
the language, te reo Māori.

Hoani Waititi, Māori language advocate and writer
of *Te Rangatahi* texts for learning Māori, teaching
in the 1950s.

Māori language petition being delivered to Parliament 1972 - *Archives New Zealand/Te Rua Mahara o te Kāwanatanga*

Ngā Tamatoa initiated a nationwide petition calling for the inclusion of te reo in primary and secondary schools. The Māori Language Petition eventually gathered 30,000 signatures.

Archives New Zealand
Te Rua Mahara o te Kāwanatanga

Archives New Zealand
Te Rua Mahara o te Kāwanatanga

over the plight of Māori lands, culture, language and people and asserted that more immediate and direct steps were needed. It was from this energy that Ngā Tamatoa arose. Conference deliberations helped to define their goals some of which included opposing racism, campaigning for Māori culture and language, seeking redress for the loss of Māori land, and ensuring Pākehā and the Crown properly observed the Treaty of Waitangi.

Some of Ngā Tamatoa's greatest achievements can be seen in the Māori language and education initiatives that exist today. Together with the Te Reo Māori Society, Ngā Tamatoa initiated a nationwide petition calling for the inclusion of te reo in primary and secondary schools. The Māori Language Petition eventually gathered 30,000 signatures. On 14 September 1972, which was announced as the inaugural Māori Language Day, it was hand-delivered to Parliament by a delegation of key supporters. As a direct result of this action the Government introduced the teaching of Māori in primary and secondary schools, although largely as an optional extra. Taking the advice of its petitioners, it also established a one-year training course for native speakers to address the shortfall in qualified staff. The Government subsequently got behind Māori Language Day, which was later expanded to Māori Language Week.

Overall, it was a great achievement, though it came at great cost. Hana Jackson was a leading figure in both Ngā Tamatoa and the Māori language campaign. She worked tirelessly, and did so in the face of Pākehā and Māori animosity. As the campaign progressed, alongside several others, Ngā Tamatoa developed a reputation for radicalism and aggression. Members experienced ridicule, personal harassment, and rejection. They were scorned by many Māori, who felt they were somehow bringing Māoridom into disrepute. They were criticised for adopting Pākehā protest methods, and chastised for being out of touch with their people and being unable to speak the language themselves. But they were mostly young and urban, and therefore belonged to the section of Māori society that felt most distanced from their culture. It now seems appropriate that those who felt most deprived of te reo should be the ones who sought support to ensure its survival.

Whatever people thought of Ngā Tamatoa and their tactics, they did succeed where others had previously failed. Furthermore, in the wake of the petition Māori continued to press for official support for the language, as well as developing their own initiatives. Continuing protests called for proper pronunciation in broadcast media, Māori programmes, more Māori people on TV and greater recognition of Māori as the language of the tangata whenua. In 1978 Ruātoki School became New Zealand's first bilingual school. This move was followed in quick succession by the establishment of the Te Atārangi movement – designed to restore te reo amongst

Te Reo Māori demonstration outside TVNZ studios at Avalon, Lower Hutt, 1977 - *Dominion Post*

March demanding equal status for Māori language in Wellington 1980 - *Dominion Post Collection, Alexander Turnbull Library*

Māori adults – Te Whare Wānanga o Raukawa at Ōtaki in 1981, and the first kōhanga reo at Wainuiomata and Waiwhetu in 1982. The kōhanga reo movement, later joined by kura kaupapa Māori and other forms of Māori immersion education, has played a primary role in revitalising the reo. The notion of Māori-language schools has attracted its share of critics – those who view such moves as separatist and others who assume all-Māori education is unhelpful to children who will have to eventually rejoin a system dominated by the English language. For Māori, the results speak for themselves: language learning also ensures the continuance of cultural imperatives – values, beliefs, tikanga.

The welfare of the language has remained at the forefront of Māori issues. In 1986, the Waitangi Tribunal reported on a claim lodged by Huirangi Waikerepuru and Ngā Kaiwhakapūmau i te Reo that alleged the Crown had failed to protect the Māori language, and had implemented policies that actively contributed to its decline.[9] The tribunal's *Te Reo Māori Report* did not go as far as the claimants had hoped, and the government response did not go as far as the tribunal had recommended. But the Māori Language Act 1987 made Māori an official language of New Zealand and allowed Māori to be spoken in any legal proceedings. The act also set up Te Taura Whiri i te Reo Māori to actively promote the reo and to guide government as it gave the newly official language practical effect. Progress in Māori education continued, as official recognition was granted to kura kaupapa Māori and wānanga. However, dissatisfaction with broadcasting policies continued, especially when Government began to restructure the broadcasting sector in the late 1980s. The Māori view was often criticised on the grounds that Māori were claiming radio frequencies which did not exist in 1840. The argument was somewhat misguided. It was clear that radio and television could have a mammoth impact on Māori-language development, taking Māori music, language, news and events into homes, schools and workplaces all over the country. Broadcast seemed one of the most potent avenues through which the Government could protect and enhance te reo. Eventually the Government did reserve broadcast frequencies for use by Māori, and in 1993 it established Te Māngai Pāho, a funding agency for the promotion of Māori language and culture.

Advances have been made since the 1972 petition broke the first ground, and they have come with more than their fair share of obstacles and controversies. A small number of Māori and Māori-language programmes are now broadcast on mainstream TV, including the staples *Te Karere* and *Marae*, and a selection of children and youth shows. The Māori Television Service is free-to-air in some parts of the country. It began broadcasting eight years after the Aotearoa Television Network closed after running a short-term trial in Auckland. Most, if not all, areas have at least one iwi or Māori radio station to tune into. Some concerns remain about the quality of the reo spoken, the level and extent of fluency, and its long-term future. Although healthier than it was thirty or forty years ago, and no longer facing its own demise, te reo Māori is still in a delicate condition, kept alive by a genuine passion for learning, and a confidence it seems to evoke in its students.

Opening of Te Kura Kaupapa Māori o Hoani Waititi, Auckland 1985 - Gil Hanly

Classes at Te Kura Kaupapa Māori o Hoani Waititi, Auckland - Gil Hanly

The Te Kōhanga Reo movement, kura kaupapa Māori and other forms of Māori immersion education, have played a primary role in revitalising te reo Māori. One of the first kura kaupapa Māori was opened at Hoani Waititi marae in 1985.

Te Upoko o te Ika, Wellington 1988 - *Dominion Post Collection, Alexander Turnbull Library*

Te Upoko o te Ika, Wellington 1988 - *Dominion Post Collection, Alexander Turnbull Library*

Te Upoko o Te Ika – Wellington's Māori radio station – began broadcasting in 1988 with an uncertain future and no guaranteed funding.

Launch of Māori television, Auckland 2004 - *Māori Television Service*

Launch of Māori television, Auckland 2004 - *Māori Television Service*

Broadcasting is one of the most potent avenues through which the government could support te reo Māori. Radio and television provides a mammoth opportunity to impact on Māori language by taking Māori music, language and news into homes, schools and workplaces all over the country.

Launch of Māori television, Auckland 2004 -*Māori Television Service*

Chapter Four
Ka Whawhai Tonu Mātou

If the blood of our people only had been spilled,
and the land remained,
then this trouble would have been over long ago.

(Tamati Ngapora, 1872)

ONE OF THE MOST COGENT MOVEMENTS OF MĀORI ACTIVISM IN the 1970s was that which rallied around land rights. It included the Māori Land March of 1975, flanked by pivotal occupations at Raglan and Bastion Point. While critiquing the 1967 Māori Affairs Amendment Act, Māori disaffection was reminded of the detrimental qualities of other legislation. The Public Works Act 1928 had featured in the taking of land at both Raglan and Bastion Point. The 1967 Rating Act enabled local authorities to alienate Māori land on which unpaid rates had accumulated, taking unfair advantage of Māori shifting to towns and cities. Parts of the Town and Country Planning Act had the effect of restricting Māori land development, while allowing other developments that paid no regard to Māori opinion and prior relationships with the lands concerned.

That land was so paramount amongst the many issues facing Māori is unsurprising. Land alienation had been high on the list of concerns Māori had aired at the many deliberations surrounding the treaty at the time of its signing. The principle of pupuri whenua had permeated and even driven many iwi and Māori organisations from the 1850s onwards, and petitioning against unjust land dealings and confiscations has been an historical facet of the Māori relationship with government. Some relief arrived in the 1920s when the Government finally began to investigate some of the major grievances, including claims to the Rotorua and Taupō lakes, confiscated lands, and later, surplus and vested lands. Settlements for these claims usually took the form of sums of money paid to Māori trust boards. Some flaws would later show in these early attempts at redress. None had considered the Treaty of Waitangi in their inquiries and negotiations and as creatures of statute the boards were not necessarily designed for long-term effectiveness and responsiveness. They were challenged by the pressures of inflation and the rising cost of living, and the benefits of their settlements had to be distributed to a rapidly increasing population. Also, the district-wide approach taken in several cases, which grouped collectives of iwi, would later have to face debate and new preferences about iwi representation and organisation. No area had

Tuaiwa (Eva) Rickard at Raglan - *Marti Friedlander Archive, on loan from the artist to Auckland Art Gallery Toi o Tamaki,*

all of its grievances heard or settled and rumblings about land loss continued. From 1985 the Waitangi Tribunal could consider treaty-based claims dating back to 1840, and the door was opened for comprehensive investigation of historical land claims all over the country. But the cumbersome claims process did not completely curtail the land-rights movement, as localised occupations and other protests in the 1990s would show.

Foremost amongst the land-rights campaigns of the 1970s was Raglan. In 1972, led by the prominent activist Tuaiwa (Eva) Rickard, the Tainui Awhiro people began an earnest drive to dispute the local council's ownership of the Raglan Golf Course and seek its return. Typically, the injustice and the sense of grievance surrounding it were long-standing. It had begun during World War Two when the Department of Civil Aviation, with the help of the Raglan County Council, used the Public Works Act to take land surrounding Miria Te Kakara meeting house and marae for an emergency airstrip. The whole community was displaced, forced to leave their homes, marae, large kūmara cultivations and urupā. As required by law some compensation was paid, but many refused to accept the government's money. The kuia Herepo Rongo called it 'black pennies', the money of corruption.[10] Small consolation could be taken from a promise that the land would be returned at the end of the war, and that no harm would befall the urupā. However, anticipating future problems, Eva Rickard's father exhumed the body of a daughter and re-interred her closer to his home. At the end of the war the portent of his action was made clear; instead of returning the land to Tainui Awhiro the Government gave it to the council, who in turn leased it to the Raglan Golf Club. One act broke two promises. Not only did people face the prospect that they had lost their homes and marae permanently, they would also soon be watching golf balls fly over their urupā.

The Raglan Golf Course eventually covered sixty-three of the eighty-eight acres the Government had originally taken. The marae and houses were levelled without any reference to their owners. Some access to a four-acre kūmara garden was retained, although only temporarily. The two urupā resisted development, and as golf course bunkers they were able to remain, disturbed but mostly intact. Tainui Awhiro was offered £330 in compensation for their loss, which they refused to accept, preferring the return of their lands in full.

In 1972 Eva accepted the dying wishes of her mother and took up the cause that had dogged her parents' generation. She began a submission-writing and petitioning effort. Seeking the full return of the land to Tainui Awhiro, her battles with government, the Ministers of Māori Affairs and of Lands, Raglan County Council and Raglan Golf Club thrust Eva into the limelight as a land-rights campaigner.[11]

Eva Rickard and the Minister of Lands Venn Young 1978 - *New Zealand Herald*

Raglan was to the fore of the land rights campaigns
of the 1970s. In 1972, the Tainui Awhiro people
under the leadership of Eva Rickard, picked up
a long-standing dispute over the local council's
ownership of the Raglan Golf Course.

In 1975 Eva joined Te Roopu o Te Matakite and played a leading role in the Land March that same year. Being on the march enabled her to network with other protest groups, and enlist support for her own cause. Later that year, she occupied the golf course and was arrested, her subsequent prosecution overturned on appeal. In 1976, with support from Te Matakite, Tainui Awhiro marched on the golf course. Their protest focussed on desecration of the urupā. After karakia, and acknowledgement of the violation that had occurred against their ancestors, the group then proceeded to fence off the urupā. An erratic weather pattern followed the marchers that day. Inclement weather had closed the golf course. But as they gathered at a local marae that morning the protest group was bathed in sunshine. Yet a torrent so heavy as to drown out the speechmaking began the instant the group entered the wharenui. As they left the marae and headed to the golf course the rain subsided again, and stayed away until the protest action was complete and the marchers were back in the comfort of the marae. When the rain returned that afternoon, it came in a theatrical downpour accompanied by thunder and lightning. The weather was proof of the rectitude of the kaupapa, and the reassurance of the ancestors. In the court case that followed, it was agreed that the land ought to be returned, but that Tainui Awhiro should pay for it. Eva declined, refusing to pay for land that rightfully belonged to the iwi. She even turned down the Department of Māori Affairs when it attempted to defuse the situation by offering to pay for the land: buying the land with public money would make it public land.

Within two years, the golf course was occupied for a second time, by 250 protesters comprising members of Tainui Awhiro and other groups that had been involved in the Land March. Eva was arrested with sixteen others, variously members of Ngā Tamatoa, Te Matakite and the Ōrākei Māori Action Group. Eva swore she would occupy the land again if she had to. She denounced the golf club as a haven for the elite and illicit Sunday boozing. Te Matakite member Ben Matthews drew attention to the injustice of the arrests when a week later he appeared on TV playing golf, on Parliament's grounds.[12]

In the aftermath of the 1978 occupation, the Government again offered the land to Tainui Awhiro, this time for a sum of $61,300, to be paid at $2000 per annum over thirty years. The golf club would be given till the end of 2007 to vacate. It was an offer that history dictated should never be accepted. The Government reworked its position until finally, in 1983, the land now known as Whaingaroa ki te Whenua was returned to the iwi, and the golf course made way for a Kōkiri training centre, farm, and marae.[13]

The whole community was displaced, forced to leave their homes, marae, large kumara cultivations and urupā. At the end of the war instead of giving the land back to Tainui Awhiro, the government gave it to the Raglan County Council, who in turn leased it to the Raglan Golf Club.

Protest at Raglan, 1978 - John Miller

Protest at Raglan, 1978 - John Miller

Protest at Raglan, 1978 - John Miller

Protest at Raglan, 1978 - John Miller

Protest at Raglan, 1978 - John Miller

In 1983, the land now known as Whaingaroa ki te Whenua was returned to the iwi and the golf course made way for kōkiri training centres, farm and marae. A monument was built at the ancestral burial ground at Te Kopua, Whaingaroa.

Angeline Greensill at the monument at Te Kopua, Whaingaroa - *New Zealand Herald*

Chapter Five
'Not One More Acre'

We are stroking, caressing the spine of the land.
We are massaging the ricked wracked back of the land with our sore but ever-loving feet.
Hell, she loves it. The land turns over with
great delight.
We love her.
From 'Papa-Tu-A-Nuku', Hone Tuwhare

AWARENESS OF HISTORICAL LAND LOSSES, AND MOBILISATION against continuing losses, grew in the shadow of the land grab authorised by the Māori Affairs Amendment Act 1967. Yet by 1975 it appeared that government legislation continued to undermine Māori rights and land tenure, and a mix of historical and contemporary issues engaged the land-rights movement. Various iwi and protest groups, including the Tainui Awhiro at Raglan, looked to each other for support as they contended with government and local authorities. Around the country, iwi were diligently trying to have land issues addressed with both central government and local authorities. Many cases dated back to the land confiscations of the 1860s, as well as unfulfilled government promises and questionable land transactions of the nineteenth century. Other wrongs were more recent, often concerning extraction of natural resources or local body encroachments on Māori land for public purposes.

It was one incident amongst a myriad that called Whina Cooper to action in 1975. Some of her children had interests in Māori land on the coast at Ngunguru northeast of Whāngārei. She had been spending time there in the early 1970s after the Whāngārei County Council designated a strip of coastline public reserve. The twenty-metre strip ran for thirty kilometres. Nearly ninety percent of the land involved belonged to the local Ngāti Wai, the remainder belonged to Pākehā owners. Ngāti Wai felt the council unfairly targeted their land because it was Māori-owned, and set up the Ngāti Wai Retention Committee to lobby for the protection of their coastal properties. The committee found a powerful ally in Whina, and she would later lead them on the Land March.[14] Whina had undertaken her first protest action at the age of eighteen near her home at Whakarapa (now Panguru), when a local Pākehā farmer began draining mudflats he was leasing from the Marine Department. The mudflats were a well-used source of seafood for local Māori, and Whina and others of her generation obstructed the farmers' drainage attempts. The matter was resolved when the department withdrew the farmer's lease. Whina had had a varied career: teacher, storekeeper, farmer. She was a commanding leader who became the first national president of the Māori Women's Welfare League in 1951.

Whina Cooper and mokopuna Irene begin Māori Land March 1975 - *New Zealand Herald*

Māori Land March, Te Hāpua 1975 - Christian Heinegg

Hangi for Māori Land March, Porirua 1975 - *Dominion Post Collection, Alexander Turnbull Library*

The 1975 Māori Land March wove together many land issues from around the country

By 1975 the many specific land issues taking shape around the country were weaving together. In March, reading the mood of the people and responding to the kōrero of earlier meetings, Whina chaired a hui at Te Puea Marae in Māngere. The hui was well-attended by a range of representatives of iwi and other interest groups, conservative and radical alike. Attention was drawn to the plight of Māori who had been rendered landless, and a call was made for the return of lands unjustly taken and a halt to any further loss of land. The role of legislation in land-taking was discussed, and the processes of remits and written submissions condemned as ineffectual. The hui agreed there was a need for more direct action. Land loss was a cause that united Māori and one that could help focus Pākehā attention on the many grievances at hand. The suggestion that a march to parliament be organised, beginning at Te Hāpua in the Far North, was taken up. The hui formalised the group Te Roopu o te Matakite and appointed Whina its leader. Such a march had been seen three years earlier in the 'Trail of Broken Treaties', the Native American land march on Washington DC. However, a Māori precedent had been set in 1867 when Riwha Titokowaru – the remarkable military leader who came to prominence during the wars in Taranaki in the 1860s – led a hīkoi of peace through the Taranaki and Wanganui districts in 1867.

Setting up Te Matakite was practically as great a feat as the march itself. It was a synergy of old and new ideologies and methods, which unified a range of groups and interests: kuia, kaumātua and rangatahi, young urban activists and older conservative traditionalists. In the six months leading up to the hui, alliances were cultivated with iwi, the Kīngitanga, the Māori council, Ngā Tamatoa, the league,

Māori Land March, Otoko Pā 1975 - *Dominion Post Collection, Alexander Turnbull Library*

Māori Land March, Porirua 1975 - John Miller.

trade unions, socialist organisations, churches and the anti-apartheid movement. The considerable support of Pākehā sent the message that Māori were not the only ones who were fed up with racial discrimination and unjust laws in Aotearoa. The mammoth task of organisation included raising funds, planning the route, negotiating with host marae, organising a petition, and recruiting support from around the country. As well as taking care of the practical details, Te Matakite also developed its platform and meaning. A carved pouwhenua, traditionally used to mark a tribe's territorial mana, was to be carried at the head of the march. Laden with the concerns of the day, its bearers were to ensure that it never touched the ground to symbolise the vast area of Māori land lost. A Memorial of Rights was also prepared and was to be presented to Prime Minister Bill Rowling on the steps of Parliament. The memorial demanded that all statutes that could alienate, designate or confiscate Māori land be repealed, and that the control of the last remaining tribal lands be vested in Māori in perpetuity. It was kept protectively in a leather-bound box, and taken out each night of the march and discussed and signed by the local kuia and kaumātua and

Māori Land March on motorway, Johnsonville 1975 - Christian Heinegg

The march planned to cover 700 miles in thirty days, making its way down the centre of the North Island, and visiting 25 marae along its route. A core group of 50 would walk the entire distance while others travelled in support vehicles.

Māori Land March, Auckland 1975 - Christian Heinegg

any distinguished guests in attendance. Eventually over 200 rangatira representing all iwi of Aotearoa signed the memorial.

After months of preparation the march left Te Hāpua on 14 September, the first day of Māori Language Week. Whina Cooper very famously took the first steps hand in hand with her mokopuna Irene. The march planned to cover 700 miles in thirty days, making its way down the centre of the North Island, and visiting twenty-five marae along its route. A core group of fifty would walk the entire distance while others travelled in support vehicles. Most supporters joined the march as it passed through their home districts, or on the final day for the march on Parliament. The petition was signed by 60,000 people and estimates of the number of Māori and Pākehā who participated throughout the month ranged from 30,000 to 40,000.

Not all Māori approved of Te Matakite. Support for it waxed and waned at different points, although the trend was towards an overall increase as the marchers headed south. At Auckland thousands of people met the marchers to join them in their historic walk over the Harbour Bridge, with Joe Hawke of Ngāti Whātua bearing the pouwhenua. Matiu Rata saw their actions as an affront to his efforts as Minister of Māori Affairs.

Māori Land March, Wellington 1975 - John Miller

Since taking office in 1972 he had been working towards reforms that would restore and fortify Māori control of Māori land, and protect against further loss. He did so while also struggling to increase his department's annual budget, which had been in steady decline since the mid-1960s. Although not widely known amongst the public, Rata had facilitated the return of some Crown lands, and intended to return more, and had written off debts that his department had accumulated against Māori land that it was responsible for farming. But his efforts came too late. With the march imminent Rata had to deal with his own sense of sorrow that it would start at his home town. But by the end of the first day, a telegram expressing his good wishes had arrived to meet the marchers at Te Kao.

For many of the participants, bruises, blisters and aches became less important as the march provided a profound cultural, spiritual and political reawakening. Those who felt distanced from their culture were able to immerse themselves in it nightly at each of the host marae. Discussions between tangata whenua and manuhiri mulled over the purpose of the march and the petition, and allowed iwi to air their own local grievances. Whether it had set out to be or not, the march was an important

John Miller

John Miller

A Memorial of Rights was prepared to be presented to Prime Minister Bill Rowling on the steps of Parliament 1975.

consciousness-raising exercise. And when it reached Wellington on 13 October 1975 an estimated 5,000 people walked the streets to Parliament in an outstanding show of support. During the speeches that followed in Parliament's grounds, the Memorial of Rights was presented to Bill Rowling who assured the crowd their trek had not been in vain. His words were not enough for a group of about sixty protesters led by Ngā Tamatoa, who set up a Māori embassy on the steps of Parliament even after Whina had told the marchers to disperse and await an outcome. The group refused to move, until they were evicted two months later. Meanwhile, another body of marchers led by Dun Mihaka went on to march around the East Cape, visiting communities they had missed on the way to Wellington. People who had been involved with Te Matakite were divided over what had transpired. Some supported Whina, others Ngā Tamatoa, and each division claimed the other was unrepresentative. Reconciliation was attempted, and the People's Union explained the situation as a widening of the political front by evolving into two distinct consciousness-raising activities. But what the public saw was a public spat caused by petty factionalism. Regardless of the internal differences, the fundamental commitment to having Māori land grievances addressed remained. In the few years following the march, people from both sides of the argument made oral and written submissions to relevant select committees and continued to support individual struggles, like those at Raglan and Bastion Point.

The aftermath of the march is often viewed with some regret, but bringing together such a disparate collection of groups and interests, even for a short time, is a huge accomplishment rarely achieved, and testament to the depth of feeling about the land issue. The conduct of the march itself cannot be faulted; its dignity has made a permanent impression on New Zealand's history.

John Miller

John Miller

Christian Heinegg

Chapter Six
Bastion Point is Māori Land

He aha te hau e wawa ra, e wawa ra?
He tiu, he raki, he tiu, he raki
Nana i a mai te puputara ki uta
E tikina e au te kotiu
Koia te pou whakairo ka tu ki Waitemata
Ka tu ki Waitemata i oku wairangi e
E tu nei, e tu nei!
(Titahi, c. 1780, predicting the arrival of Pākehā in Auckland)

IN LATE 1976 ROBERT MULDOON'S NATIONAL GOVERNMENT announced plans to subdivide and sell twenty-four hectares of Crown land at Bastion Point on Auckland's Waitematā Harbour – prime real estate. Early the following year the Ōrākei Māori Committee Action Group, led by Joe Hawke, shifted onto the land and began a seventeen-month occupation that would end in their being forcibly evicted. The Ngāti Whātua claims to Bastion Point, also known to Māori as Takaparawha, are an example of the longevity of many Māori grievances, and the way that they can become layered one upon the other over time.[15]

Back in the 1840s and 1850s the local chiefs could not have predicted, and certainly did not intend, that colonisation would render future generations homeless in their own land. In 1840 the Ngāti Whātua chief, Apihai Te Kawau, entered an agreement with Governor Hobson that provided the 3,000 acres on which Auckland quickly grew. He is the unremembered founder of Auckland, a formidable economic power who took full advantage of the flourishing centre of commercial activity at his doorstep. And he was a generous patron. Alliances with the Anglican Church saw him gift land for a church and school site – which the church sold in later years. And the Ōrākei headland became Crown land for defence purposes in 1859, amidst Government fears for national security. But Ngāti Whātua of Ōrākei essentially controlled these transactions, and expected the land to be returned when it no longer fulfilled the purpose for which it was given. Moreover, as early as 1840 they had made it clear that their 700-acre Ōrākei block was their tribal base, never to be relinquished and utterly unattainable by the Government or anyone else. However, the certainty that they would keep Ōrākei was quickly undermined after the Native Land Court began operating.

Trig at Bastion Point 1982 - John Miller

In 1840 the Ngāti Whātua chief, Apihai te Kawau, entered an agreement with Governor Hobson that provided the 3,000 acres on which Auckland quickly grew. In 1859 the Ōrākei headland became Crown land for defence purposes. More land losses followed, and by 1928, apart from their papakāinga at Ōkahu Bay, Ngāti Whātua retained a mere three acres at Ōrākei.

Bastion Point 1977 - *New Zealand Herald*

In 1869 the court investigated the Ōrākei block and awarded ownership to thirteen individuals. Four years later the investigation was followed by the issue of a certificate of title which also declared the entire area 'absolutely inalienable'. Initially having the land vested in thirteen owners was not problematic for Ngāti Whātua, who regarded the owners as trustees. But the fact was the court had no mechanism for Māori understandings of trusteeship, and its award effectively disinherited the majority of the iwi. The long history of severing Ōrākei from its people had begun, and would find new impetus in the 1880s. In 1882 the Government unpicked the restrictions on alienation by allowing for long-term leases, and in 1886 took part of the land for more defence work. Then in 1898 the death knell rang as the court partitioned the block and divided it between the thirteen owners or their successors, reserving just forty acres at Ōkahu Bay for a papakāinga. The will of the group, which usually provided a natural safeguard against alienation of communally-owned land, was undermined by the newly fragmented ownership.

Reoccupation of Bastion Point 1982 - Gil Hanly

When the Government sold the Ōrākei headland for a subdivision, Ngāti Whātua began an occupation of the site that lasted from 6 January 1977 to 25 May 1978.

Despite protestations from Ngāti Whātua about the court's interpretation of tribal ownership, the Government began to explore the prospect of buying the block for Pākehā settlement. Meanwhile, in 1908, Ngāti Whātua's resistance found some support when a government-appointed commission found that the Ōrākei land was essentially tribal property that should never be alienated. Nonetheless, in 1913 the Crown announced its intention to buy the Ōrākei block, partly under pressure from leaseholders lobbying for the freehold. About the same time the papakāinga had come into the purview of the Auckland City Council who wanted to compulsorily acquire the settlement. As it was, in 1912 a sewerage pipe had been laid in front of the papakāinga, ignoring the objections of those who lived there. The pipe discharged untreated sewage into a bay with which Ngāti Whātua still interacted along traditional lines. It also had the effect of preventing storm water from running off properly, turning the papakāinga into a swamp for much of the year and seriously compromising people's health. The Crown's intention to purchase Ōrākei, and the council's designs on the papakāinga weighed heavily on Ngāti Whātua who did not even have tribal ownership of their lands to lean on. The Crown used orders in council to prevent the owners selling to anyone but the Government, and passed legislation to side-step the usual prerequisite of securing the approval of the majority of owners before a sale could proceed. The Crown's purchasing activity could then single out individual owners and be sustained over a period of years, regardless of how tenacious Ngāti Whātua resistance became.

When the Waitangi Tribunal reported on the Ōrākei claim in 1987 it found ample evidence that both (legal) owners and non-owners were opposed to the Crown's intention to purchase their lands. Some who sold said they were promised the papakāinga would be spared. Others sold on the understanding that house sites would be reserved from the sale. Others, it seems, may have succumbed after seeing how much land the Crown had already purchased or after being threatened with compulsory acquisition. By 1928, apart from the papakāinga, Ngāti Whātua retained a mere three acres at Ōrākei. The last interests of those who refused to sell were mopped up in 1950 using the Public Works Act, and in the meantime the Crown began wresting the papakāinga from its inhabitants. It proceeded to buy up interests, and continued to do so even after a 1939 commission pointed out a number of irregularities in the ways that land interests were conveyed to the Crown. Regardless of the title, Ngāti Whātua continued living at the Ōkahu Bay papakāinga. But the City of Auckland, the city Ngāti Whātua helped to found, said it was needed for a park. By the 1950s, the Government viewed the families who remained at Ōkahu Bay as squatters on Crown land, and their settlement insanitary. Things came to a head in 1951 when, on the pretext of protecting their health, the Crown evicted

March in support of Bastion Point reoccupation, Auckland 1982 - Gil Hanly

the remaining families and relocated them to homes in nearby streets. The efforts of Ngāti Whātua to hold fast to their tribal heartland literally went up in smoke and flame as their meeting house and homes at Ōkahu Bay were burned to the ground. In the aftermath the government set aside some land to build a marae to replace the one it had destroyed. But despite being located on the homelands of Ngāti Whātua, the marae that was eventually built became not a tribal marae but a national marae. It seems that even when there was nothing left the Crown could still find something to take from Ngāti Whātua.

When Joe Hawke began the occupation of Bastion Point, he was following a long line of previous attempts at obtaining a just hearing. Ngāti Whātua had been steadfast in their insistence the Crown should be kept out of their land. Over time numerous actions were taken to the Māori Land Court, the Supreme Court, the Court of Appeal and the Compensation Court. The people appeared before commissions and committees of inquiry, and petitioned Parliament, all to no avail. Prime Minister Robert Muldoon probably also followed a long line of previous official dealings with Ngāti Whātua. When he embarked on his plan to dispose of the Crown's remaining interests at Ōrākei, he did so without discussing the matter with Ngāti Whātua who

Gil Hanly

Gil Hanly

Gil Hanly

had already signalled their interest in the land as a means of resolving their claims. Work on the subdivision was to begin on 6 January 1977; the occupation began on the fourth. [16] Support came from familiar quarters: Te Matakite, Ngā Tamatoa, socialist organisations, CARE and HART, trade unions, and church leaders. Some politicians supported the protest, as did members of the Māori Battalion, and local residents opposed to the subdivision. Leaflets, press statements and public speeches highlighted the kaupapa. T-shirts, badges and posters contributed to the fundraising effort, and 20,000 people added their names to the petition that was produced. In April, a disused warehouse was dismantled and trucked to the site and became Arohanui Marae, supplemented by makeshift houses, tents and caravans. It was a living papakāinga. Fundraising events attracted top New Zealand performers. Like the Land March, participants were immersed in the tikanga of the marae and given detailed explanations of the history of the land. It was also hard work. Facilities were rudimentary and winter soon came to the exposed site. Financial hardship and the impact on family life were weighed against long-term commitment to the occupation. Nine months into the protest a tent fire tragically took the young life of Joanne Hawke. A memorial garden was planted in her name.

In February 1978, a year after the occupation began and the same month the Raglan protestors were arrested, the National Government came up with an offer that would see some land returned to Ngāti Whātua, but which would also saddle them with a debt of $200,000 to pay some of the development costs associated with the land. The offer had the effect of splitting the people. Moderate kaumātua wanted the occupiers to leave so that the offer could be negotiated within the law, and without the menace of protest. The Government felt the offer was very generous, and had difficulty hiding its disdain when Joe Hawke spurned it and remained at Bastion Point. In April the Crown took an injunction against four of the protest leaders and had an eviction notice served. On 25 May 1978 the Bastion Point protestors came face to face with 600 police and army officers, there to forcibly remove them. But Bastion Point was a peaceful protest. Supporters were told they were free to leave if they wanted to avoid arrest. Those who stayed were encouraged to resist without aggression. Still,

Reoccupation of Bastion Point, confrontation with police 1982 - Gil Hanly

when the police and army moved in, 222 people were arrested, and the marae that had been their home for 506 days was demolished and carted away. All that remained was a lonely tree, planted in the memorial garden for Joanne Hawke.

By year's end, the Government's offer was made a fait accompli. For the price of $200,000 the Orakei Block (Vesting and Use) Act returned thirteen acres and twenty-seven state houses to the newly constituted Ōrākei Māori Trust Board. But while the occupation had ended, the protest had not. Attention turned to the court cases that ensued. Defendants and their supporters marched from Takaparawha to court. Delaying tactics were used to great effect in an effort to slow proceedings, which supporters disrupted with cries of 'Bastion Point is Māori Land' from the public gallery. Eventually, the Governor General declared a stay on proceedings. The 180 cases yet to be prosecuted were dismissed. Those who had already been convicted appealed, and all the convictions were dropped in 1979. But neither the protest nor its arrests died; in 1982, two re-occupations of Bastion Point occurred. The first resulted in eleven arrests, the second in more than 100.

The Ōrākei claim became the first of the historical claims to be heard by the Waitangi Tribunal. In its 1987 report the tribunal recommended the return of Bastion Point to its rightful owners.

Having remained aloof from the Crown's 1978 settlement, Joe Hawke took a claim to the Waitangi Tribunal after its jurisdiction was amended to deal with claims retrospectively. With Joe Hawke at the helm, the Ōrākei claim became the first of the historical claims the tribunal heard. In its 1987 report the tribunal recommended the return of Bastion Point to its rightful owners. In summary, the tribunal found what the claimants had insisted for generations: the Crown had failed to uphold the tribal ownership which Ngāti Whātua o Ōrākei clearly preferred, and arising from that mismanagement of Māori land tenure the Crown had gone on to contravene the treaty in acquiring the land at Ōrākei, evicting the people from Ōkahu Bay, destroying their settlement, and gifting what ought to have been their new marae to the nation. However the tribunal also gave both Joe Hawke and the Crown something of a reprimand. Those who had occupied Takaparawha, the tribunal said, were in breach of the treaty because they acted outside the law, although there were mitigating circumstances. And in the tribunal's assessment of the 1978 settlement, the reparation was limited to the land taken under the Public Works Act and not the full range of grievances Ngāti Whātua bore. A settlement more comprehensive than that arranged in 1978 followed in 1991 and what could be restored of the Ngāti Whātua stronghold at Ōrākei, has been. The civic-mindedness that began the Ngāti Whātua relationship with the City of Auckland has also been rebuilt, their ties with the council bringing the iwi shared responsibility for public places in their area.

Often remembered for the scenes of confrontation associated with the occupation, Takaparawha is one of the hallmarks of modern activism. Like other land protests of recent decades it lifted itself out of the sluggish morass of suits, submissions and petitions and chose direct action instead. It was a hard-fought campaign – long, complex and imbued with a poignancy difficult to express.

Waitangi Tribunal at Ōrākei 1986 - Gil Hanly

Chapter Seven
Maranga Mai

FROM THE LATE 1970S AND INTO THE 1980S A PROLIFERATION of protest organisations joined the land rights movement in populating the Māori political landscape. New groups merged and networked with old, mobilising around Waitangi Day actions, anti-apartheid and anti-racism movements, and a profusion of event-specific protests. The Waitangi Action Committee (WAC), He Taua, the Māori People's Liberation Movement of Aotearoa, the Māori Women's Movement, and Hui Tāne kept themselves − not to mention the police, the press and public opinion − politically busy. Waitangi Day protests begun by Ngā Tamatoa became a permanent fixture on the protest calendar, culminating in the 1984 Hīkoi ki Waitangi. Also in 1984 two provocative additions to the nation's literary culture were published. Donna Awatere, already identified by Robert Muldoon as a subversive, published *Maori Sovereignty*, a book notorious for condemning 'white hatred' for its role in the ills that plagued Māori society and advocating Māori sovereignty. And Dun Mihaka challenged both the law and the Crown with his book *Whakapohane*. In the meantime, Matiu Rata resigned, first from the Labour Party and then from Parliament. Disillusioned, he was no longer willing to tolerate the blinkered one-people idealism of government policy, pointing to the continued social and economic deprivation of Māori and official apathy toward Māori aspirations. Rata's resignation forced a by-election in June 1980, and his ensuing campaign attracted considerable activist support. Although he did not win he did establish his new Mana Motuhake party as a political strength that seriously threatened the Labour Party's long history of monopolising the Māori vote.

Māori activism brought the Treaty of Waitangi to the centre of a public conversation which was now pushed to broaden its analysis and consider the treaty's past

MAORI SOVEREIGNTY

DONNA AWATERE

The late 1970s and 1980s saw a proliferation
of protest organisations. New groups merged and
networked with old, mobilizing around Waitangi Day
actions, anti-apartheid and anti-racism movements,
and a profusion of event-specific protests.

Waitangi Day protest, Wellington 1986 - Gil Hanly

Waitangi Day protest, Wellington 1986 - Gil Hanly

Waitangi Day protest, Wellington 1986 - Gil Hanly

Some challenges became important to Pākehā, particularly those surrounding debate about identity which had emanated from debates about the treaty. Pākehā were challenged to learn about themselves – their own culture, identity, and history.

as well as its practical standing and effect in modern society. Māori autonomy, self-determination, sovereignty, independence and mana motuhake all added to the vernacular of tino rangatiranga. Calls were made to face the historically fraudulent handling of the treaty, and to ratify and honour it. Māori women drew attention to their distinct position in society, and the double-dose of discrimination they faced when sexism and racism joined forces. Māori artists, writers and musicians released the spirit and drive of the evolving debate into their works. New bottom lines were constantly being laid down.

Māori activists were often portrayed as an obnoxious minority haranguing the country with unrealistic and unfounded demands. But some challenges became important to Pākehā. In an acknowledgement that understanding ourselves is an access to understanding each other, Pākehā were challenged to learn about themselves – their own culture, identity, and history. Māori activists and their supporters also challenged themselves. Māori identity was debated and expressions of it explored, encouraging participation in the Māori cultural renaissance that was underway. Māori activism also identified a breach in the opportunities to learn Māori politics and history and offered a curriculum distributed through newsletters, leaflets, badges, T-shirts, education kits, workshops, hui, music, art and poetry, all produced in alignment with the protesting voice.

While modern activism maintained its use of cutting-edge direct action, interactions with the State developed on other fronts, and the Government's Māori policy gradually began to respond to new influences.[17] Kara Puketapu became the Secretary of Māori Affairs in 1977, a post he held till 1983. It was only the second time a Māori had held the position, yet the department's antecedents could be traced back to 1840. Kara was aware of the undercurrent of discontent that young Māori activists represented, and also understood the socioeconomic situation of Māori. Amongst his aims

In July 1973 the first conference of writers and artists was held at Te Kaha. Two hundred carvers, writers, painters, musicians, actors, singers, sculptors, photographers, film-makers, poets and dancers gathered.

John Miller

John Miller

John Miller

Opening of Tū Tangata strategy conference at Parliament 1980 - *Dominion Post Collection, Alexander Turnbull Library*

was a shift to a new philosophy of Māori development under the banner *Tū Tangata* which would recognise the strength of Māori people and harness their energies with the resources of the department. The shift continued under the fourth Labour government when the 1984 Hui Taumata, a Māori economic summit, launched a decade of Māori development. Tribal organisations would be strengthened, selected government programmes devolved to them, and new iwi-based social and economic initiatives encouraged.

These policy developments are usually coupled with changes to the Waitangi Tribunal's legislation to explain a simultaneous downturn in protest activity. But the results of the changes occurring within the bureaucracy were not immediately apparent, and may only offer a partial explanation. Other possible explanations included a trend amongst some urban Māori to return to their mainly rural and provincial tribal heartlands. People had families, partook of some of the incoming developments like kōhanga reo, and involved themselves in their iwi treaty claims and other resolutions of grievance. After all, Māori activism is synonymous with multi-tasking adaptability, and public attention is not a measure of its being, no matter how much the headlines love Māori protest. Amongst the many headline-makers, though, were a confrontation between the engineering students of the University of Auckland and He Taua in 1979, and the 1980 tour of the theatrical group Maranga Mai. [18]

Opening of Tū Tangata strategy conference at Parliament 1980 - *Dominion Post Collection, Alexander Turnbull Library*

Kara Puketapu, as Secretary of Māori Affairs in 1977, developed a shift to a new philosophy of Māori development under the banner *Tū Tangata.*

The account of the violent confrontation that took place between He Taua and the engineering students adhered to a pattern all too familiar to the protest movement. The head-to-head conflict that defined the incident only came after years of pursuing official channels with no tangible result. Also, more moderate responses and strategies came in on the tide of public condemnation that typically hounded the protestors in the aftermath. The university – despite its dedication to academic pursuits and the training of future leaders – had become home to an insulting and culturally abusive mock haka. By the 1970s the mock haka had become something of a tradition with engineering students who performed it with great drunken relish as a part of their annual capping celebrations. Even if Māori forgave the engineers' for their penchant for cultural appropriation, the haka was still highly offensive. The students dressed in grass skirts and painted obscenities on their bodies, including male genitalia and insults to women. The all-Pākehā all-male 'haka party' would then perform a haka that referred to Māori as a source of 'the pox' and repeatedly used the popular racist slur,

Race Relations Conciliators at Auckland University wait to address students 1979 - Gil Hanly

'Hori'. Māori and Pacific Island students, including an undergraduate Pat Hohepa, had begun using the university's official channels to voice their disapproval from the end of the 1950s. In 1971, a letter from Ngā Tamatoa's Syd Jackson asked the Auckland University Students' Association to renounce the haka. While the representative student bodies did distance themselves from it, the haka continued. In the lead-up to their grave error of judgement, the engineering students chose to ignore a mounting record of complaint, including a disapproving letter from the usually conservative Māori Club urging the engineering students to meet and discuss the matter before performing the haka again.

The students were undeterred. On 1 May 1979, as they prepared for their annual day of revelry and emboldened by the mandatory keg of beer, they were interrupted by a group of twenty-one Māori and Pacific Island men and women demanding they remove their grass skirts. A scuffle broke out in which thirteen students claimed they were assaulted. The entire episode lasted less than five minutes. The protestors left once they were satisfied they had achieved their goal of removing the skirts. In a press release later that day, using the name He Taua, they took responsibility for the

Protestors waiting outside Auckland District Court 1979 - Gil Hanly

The violent confrontation between the engineering
students of Auckland University and He Taua only
came after years of pursuing official channels with
no tangible result.

Maranga Mai performing in 1980 - John Miller

incident. Within hours eleven members of He Taua were at Auckland Central Police Station charged with rioting, and on the receiving end of police wrath. Charges of injuring with intent were later laid, although He Taua maintained their only goal was to get the students to remove the skirts.

In the weeks that followed misinformation and sensationalism overshadowed attempts to contextualise the event in terms of a general and ongoing failure in society to face and resolve long-standing Māori grievances. He Taua was branded an over-sensitive, rampaging gang, unable to take the light-hearted prank of students who were the innocent victims of an unprovoked attack. Pressure was put on Māori leaders to condemn He Taua. It took a month for the press to admit the existence of Māori support, which was widespread but usually came with the proviso that violence should not be condoned. Respected, expert and moderate older leaders maintained a presence in the subsequent five-day trial. Alongside the younger activists, they were able to present a broader perspective of what occurred and why, and an explanation of the cultural violation that the students' haka represented. But the deliberations of the courtroom could not undo the dangerous first impressions created by the headlines and public persecution that dogged He Taua.

Though Judge Blackwood ruled out cultural insult as a defence, he was aware of the political implications of the case. Of the total eighty-eight charges laid, most were dismissed. Seven of the eleven charged were convicted of participating in a riot and five of injury with intent. The defendants were sentenced to periodic detention, although imprisonment for up to fourteen years was a real possibility. In his judgement, Blackwood said that the engineering students' actions were unjustifiable in a multicultural society, but did not warrant the 'lynch law' that He Taua chose to practise.

Sensing a racial divide was forming, the Human Rights Commission called for submissions on racial harmony. In 1980 the results of more than 400 submissions were published. The commission's analysis of the submissions was published in a second report, *Race Against Time*. For a while, *Race Against Time* influenced government policy on race relations as it tried to find a path towards multiculturalism, which many people said could only be found by first achieving biculturalism. But even as the commission stepped in to treat the race-relations headache that He Taua had diagnosed, Maranga Mai was already on the road to notoriety with their own brand of politically astute music and drama.

Maranga Mai was a performance group from the Hokianga. Their play of the same name was an adaptation of a script previously performed by members of He Taua. The troupe had been involved in a number of the protests of the 1970s, and if they lacked formal training and experience it was more than made up for by their passion and commitment. The play dramatised the events of the 1970s, proclaiming the period the dawning of the age of Māori awareness. An example of the politicisation of Māori arts, Maranga Mai made clever and artistic use of music and protest lyrics as a vehicle for getting through a performance which many audiences found harrowing. Some parts emphasised discrimination in the justice system and the stand-over tactics of police, language that could offend was frequently used, and a Pākehā policeman was shot in the closing scenes. After two weeks' practice and an impromptu performance at a family gathering Maranga Mai hit the road, with no money, inadequate transport and no formal itinerary. Their first public performance at the Maidment Theatre in Auckland enabled them to obtain a reasonable vehicle, and they continued touring schools and Māori venues around the North Island. Reactions to the play were mixed. There was some support for the theatrical commentary on Māori land issues and injustices, but there were reservations about its delivery. Controversy set in after a performance to pupils at Mangere College in May 1980. A barrage of complaints from parents and teachers led to a bureaucratic investigation into the members of Maranga Mai, and the youth worker who had organised the performance, Brian Lepou, who had also been involved with He Taua, faced the prospect of dismissal. Maranga Mai were accused of inciting racial disharmony, and their performance described as crude, offensive and extremely militant, deserving of the contempt with which it was treated. More sympathetic critiques described the play as thoughtful and important social commentary, upsetting only for those who had yet to face the realities of New Zealand's racial situation.

In September, MP for Southern Māori Whetu Tirikatene-Sullivan arranged a special performance of the play at Parliament. Relatively few attended, but the troupe gave the most dynamic performance they could, taking advantage of the small number of MPs in attendance and addressing them directly as part of the play. In an unscripted moment at the very end a beer bottle was thrown against a wall. It was a dramatic reference to the kind of frustration simmering under the surface of a society that responded with complacency to an indigenous voice that felt consistently maligned and misunderstood, if not ignored. A small number who were in the audience that day were moved by what they saw, but the press chose to highlight the shock value of what it called the 'urban guerrilla' play. The usual negative attention trailed the group. The press drew attention to an arts grant Maranga Mai received to assist with their costs, and an official complaint to the race relations conciliator, which was later dismissed, alleged the group incited racial disharmony. Proving the adage that no publicity is bad publicity, Maranga Mai played to packed houses till the end of its tour, as people came to see what the fuss was about. Racism, was the issue. He Taua and Maranga Mai made that clear. And for those that missed the message, 1981 was about to provide another learning opportunity.

Bay of Plenty Times

Frustrated at the length of time taken for government to address their claims to 40,000 hectares of Tauranga land confiscated in 1864, members of Ngāi Tamarāwaho occupied the Tauranga Town Hall in September 1987.

Matt Tarawa at Tauranga
1987 - *Bay of Plenty Times*

Bay of Plenty Times

Gil Hanly

Protest camp at Maioro 1990 - Gil Hanly

Gil Hanly

Nganeko Minhinnick at Maioro 1990 - Gil Hanly

Gil Hanly

One of the Muldoon Government's economic development schemes, commonly known as 'Think Big', was the New Zealand Steel plant at Waiuku on the Manukau Harbour – lands of Ngāti Te Ata. Despite claims by Ngāti Te Ata there were extensive burial grounds on these lands, the mining company used huge excavators to mine the sands.

Chapter Eight
Rejecting Racist Rugby

RUGBY, THE ALL BLACKS: ORIGINAL, INVINCIBLE AND ON AT LEAST one occasion cavalier. Rugby, like war, has long been one of New Zealand's cultural sealants, protecting the myths of nationhood. Māori achievements on battle and rugby fields were historically held up by Pākehā as symbols of the racial accord about which they were so proud. And the haka has become synonymous with the All Blacks. Rugby's apparent immunity to race analysis means it provides the only truly level playing field in the life of the country, and has accepted parallel Māori development in the form of Māori teams, tours and tournaments for more than a century now. But in 1981 when the South African Springboks toured, and with the world watching, New Zealand was torn asunder by the very game that seemed so indivisible from the country's sense of itself.

New Zealand's rugby relationship with South Africa stretches back to the early twentieth century, and Māori exclusion from teams that toured South Africa is as old. In New Zealand, love of Māori rugby meant the Springboks did play a Māori team in 1921 and again in 1956, although amidst considerable animosity on the part of the South Africans. Opposition against sporting contacts with South Africa began to broaden throughout the 1960s and 1970s. In 1960, more than 60,000 signed the 'No Maoris, No Tour' petition, and in 1973 the Government cancelled a scheduled Springbok tour of New Zealand. International criticism of South Africa's apartheid regime also solidified, particularly after police massacred more than 360 blacks in Soweto in 1976. With the South Africans expelled from a number of international sporting bodies and other countries ending sporting contacts with them the NZRFU faced increasing pressure to stop playing the Springboks. Rising controversy failed to discourage Muldoon's government, which gave its approval to the 1976 All Black tour

March against Springbok Tour, Auckland 1981 - *Dominion Post Collection, Alexander Turnbull Library*

In 1977 Prime Minister Muldoon signed the Gleneagles Agreement objecting to sporting contacts with South Africa. Yet the 1981 Springbok tour of New Zealand was allowed to proceed. By then New Zealand's anti-tour sentiment had quietly reached its peak and polls showed public opinion was tipped against the tour.

March against Springbok Tour, Auckland 1981 - Gil Hanly

of South Africa. Twenty-one African nations responded by boycotting the Olympic Games in Montreal that year. In an attempt to stave off further international censure, Muldoon signed the 1977 Gleneagles Agreement objecting to sporting contacts with South Africa. Yet the 1981 Springbok tour of New Zealand was allowed to proceed. By then, New Zealand's anti-tour sentiment had quietly reached its peak and polls showed public opinion was tipped against the tour.

Not only had the anti-apartheid movement grown by 1981, but the Māori protest movement had matured also. The Waitangi Action Committee had sharpened the focus on the treaty, and Waitangi Day actions had increased experience with police aggression, arrest and court proceedings. Māori women were developing their own consciousness-raising efforts and analyses of the colonisation experience, which included critiques of the Māori patriarchy. Māori alliances with Pākehā activist organisations had been enduring, but were sometimes uneasy. In 1981 the Patu Squad continued the distinct Māori voice that featured in New Zealand's anti-apartheid movement. Pākehā anti-tour protestors were challenged to consider not just South Africa's apartheid, but also the racism that occurred in New Zealand's own backyard.

Anti- Springbok Tour demonstration, Wellington 1981 - *Dominion Post Collection, Alexander Turnbull Library*

Leadership for the Patu Squad was provided by some of the key 'neo-Māori activists' identified by Ranginui Walker, like Ripeka Evans, Donna Awatere and Hone Harawira. An estimated one hundred people made up the core group of the squad, complemented with other protest networks and local Māori groups at the places where matches were scheduled and demonstrations took place.[19] Māori activists were unfaltering in their opposition to the tour; Māori conservatives dithered by comparison. The Māori council officially opposed the tour. But the Tairawhiti District Māori Council dissented from that stand, and the Taitokerau district took some time to reach that position. Initially Taitokerau had publicly recommended the tour go ahead, though some individual members were opposed. Within two months, however, Taitokerau announced it was in fact opposed to the tour, especially as sporting contacts with South Africa had changed so dramatically in recent years. Hiwi Tauroa, the Race Relations Conciliator, suggested any tour should be opposed until blacks were given an equal opportunity to participate. He added that the tour distracted New Zealanders from the very important issues facing the country, such as increasing unemployment amongst Māori and Pacific Islanders.

Gil Hanly

Gil Hanly

Protest against the 1981 Springbok Tour was widespread and determined. So was support. Over a period of eight weeks, more than 150,000 New Zealanders demonstrated against the tour in twenty-eight centres. When the second game of the tour, scheduled for Hamilton, was cancelled because protestors invaded the field, rugby fans were incensed and vented their anger by hurling a mixture of abuse, beer bottles and other impromptu missiles. These volatile feelings were further intensified after police used violence against protestors in Wellington ten days into the tour. Determination on both sides became vehement and policing of the situation, provided primarily by two riot squads, served only to exacerbate the mood. Running battles between protestors, the police and rugby fans caught the attention of international media, and it looked as if New Zealand was on the brink of civil war. Spectators were required to be in the grounds at least an hour before kick off. Police set up blockades in streets surrounding the venues, donned riot gear, and used their batons against hundreds of protestors. Protestors did what they could to sabotage games, and in Auckland the third test match of the series was flour-bombed from a low-flying light plane.

By the end of the tour, almost 2,000 protestors had been arrested. Officially at least, the All Blacks and the Springboks did not play each other in rugby again until after South Africa's apartheid-supporting administration was dismantled in 1994. Unofficially, a team of All Blacks calling themselves the Cavaliers toured South Africa in 1986; other All Blacks refused. While the 1981 protests succeeded in rejecting racist rugby, some of their effects spun-off into subsequent Waitangi actions. The hardened police practices seen during the tour continued at subsequent Waitangi protests. In the years following the tour there was also a noticeable spike in active Pākehā support of Waitangi Day protests, and a growing consciousness of the treaty amongst the leadership of the Christian churches.

Gil Hanly

Anti-Springbok Tour demonstrations, Auckland 1981 - Gil Hanly

Chapter Nine
Hīkoi ki Waitangi

AS THE SEVENTIES BECAME THE EIGHTIES THE TREATY OF WAITANGI and Waitangi Day celebrations became firmly established as the focal point of Maori activism.[20] In 1979 the Waitangi Action Committee resumed the annual Waitangi protests first begun by Ngā Tamatoa. Initially, protests pushed for the Waitangi Day celebrations to be abandoned, and denounced the treaty as a fraud. Such was the cynicism of the movement that pursuing the ratification of the treaty was viewed as a wasted exercise; the cost of honest settlement of outstanding grievances was prohibitive and no government would attempt it. Over the years, however, the rhetoric settled into a general demand for the Government to honour the treaty, and a call for tino rangatiratanga or Māori independence.

In 1981 the investitures of Sir Graham Latimer and Dame Whina Cooper were targeted as a part of the Waitangi Day protests. What was essentially a peaceful although vocal and challenging protest was portrayed by police and media as a riot. Eight protestors were arrested. But the dismissal of the charges laid against them – on the grounds that police evidence failed to prove even an inkling of riotous behaviour – could not dispel the growing public perception that the protestors were a fringe group of violent troublemakers. Yet Māori activists have never been without a degree of conservative support. The National Council of Churches, for example, began to question its role in blessing a celebration which Māori clearly regarded as a celebration of the injustices perpetuated against them. Also, support could consistently be found amongst Pacific Island communities, Pākehā anti-racism and treaty education groups, tertiary students, socialists, and unionists.

The following year, the ranks of the core group of activists swelled to about 300, partly due to an increased number of Pākehā supporters in attendance. Still smarting from the events of 1981, policing was also more heavy-handed and a line of officers kept protestors back from the ceremony in the grounds of the Treaty House. Protestors heckled from behind the police line, and amongst the items thrown was an egg that hit the Governor-General Sir David Beattie. Police tactics were ratcheted up

Gil Hanly

another notch for 1983 in a return to the donning of riot gear. Almost one hundred protestors, Māori and Pākehā, were arrested before any protest even occurred. Half were arrested without getting anywhere near the treaty grounds, and half were arrested at the grounds themselves in an operation slated by the Auckland District Law Society.

Rather than quell protest activity, the hardening of police procedure seemed to have the opposite effect. In 1984 the Hīkoi ki Waitangi, from Ngāruawāhia to Waitangi, became the pinnacle of Waitangi Day activism, demonstrating the breadth and depth of Māori concerns about the treaty and the expansion of support from non-Māori organisations and individuals. The Hīkoi ki Waitangi initiated the modern-day partnership of the Kīngitanga and Te Kotahitanga, Māori political groups that dated back to the mid-nineteenth century. Veteran Māori rights activists Eva Rickard and Titewhai Harawira were appointed president and secretary of the Hīkoi respectively, and the entire undertaking received the blessing of Dame Te Atairangikaahu. Like the Land March before it, the Hīkoi unified Māori across iwi boundaries, and drew Pākehā, Pacific Islanders, young, old, conservative, liberal and radical under the common cause of the Treaty of Waitangi. Significantly, one of the stopovers on the way to Waitangi was Takaparawha, touchstone of the land rights movement. Ngāti Whātua's hosting of the Hīkoi underlined the view that Bastion Point was, indeed, Māori land.

At Waitangi, some 4,000 protestors gathered expecting to meet with the Governor-General, who had offered to meet a delegation. However, police confronted the main body of the Hīkoi at the Waitangi Bridge and stopped them from crossing. Claiming the Hīkoi could not be trusted to withdraw after meeting with Beattie, the police refused the marchers entry to the treaty grounds instead shepherding them into one of the nearby reserves and keeping them there. Despite the way in which the Hīkoi ki Waitangi concluded, the massive show of dissatisfaction with the Waitangi Day celebrations was irrefutable. Still, its deep significance was probably lost on police, politicians, and public alike. The decision to proceed or not with what could have been a grand historical moment was left in the hands of a police force known for its contempt of the Māori protest movement.

As New Zealand well knows, Waitangi Day protests have continued unabated in the intervening twenty years, despite a view that Māori activism quietened from the late 1980s. From about 1985 the Māori independence group Te Kawariki, based in the Far North, developed a critical presence at Waitangi Day celebrations, which it maintained into the twenty-first century. It also held to an education kaupapa focussing on Māori understandings of colonisation and Māori culture and identity. Heckling, disrupting official proceedings, shouting down speech-makers, and directly challenging Prime Ministers, Governors-General and other officials have commonly

Hīkoi ki Waitangi 1984 - Gil Hanly

In 1984 the Hīkoi from Ngāruawahia to Waitangi became the pinnacle of Waitangi Day activism, demonstrating the breadth and depth of Māori concerns about the treaty and the expansion of support from non-Māori organisations and individuals.

Hīkoi ki Waitangi 1984 - Gil Hanly

Hīkoi ki Waitangi 1984 - Gil Hanly

formed a major part of protest actions. Where relevant, Waitangi Day protests have also been overlaid with topical issues from the Māori agenda such as resistance to the fiscal envelope, and later the new prison proposed for Ngāwhā.

Waitangi Day protestors have most often borne the brunt of media and political backlash. Over the years, the media has enjoyed reporting on specific events such as a T-shirt thrown at the Queen, whakapohane, stomping on the New Zealand flag, the reduction of the then Leader of the Opposition Helen Clark to tears, and sometimes scuffles between protestors and the police or protestors and government officials. Attempts have been made to ban protestors from the Te Tii Marae at Waitangi, although bans against non-Māori media in recent years have been more successful. For its part, years of commemorations have seen the Government come and go from Waitangi, but not because it ever felt the day would be better spent contemplating its handling of treaty issues or calls for the recognition of tino rangatiratanga Māori. Instead, irregular government boycotts of Waitangi have been used largely as a means of punishing Māori for the perceived improprieties and insults suffered at the hands of activists. Dismissing protestors as a malcontent fringe element is another strategy both politicians and media have used to try and sideline protestors. It may be true that there is some impatience with the tactics that Māori activists prefer to employ. However the Land March, the Hīkoi ki Waitangi, and now Hīkoi 2004 have all been large but temperate reminders that the fundamental tenet of staying true to the treaty is shared across the continuum of Māori politics.

Whina Cooper, Eva Rickard, Titewhai Harawira at Waitangi 1985 - Gil Hanly

Hīkoi ki Waitangi 1984 - Gil Hanly

Hīkoi ki Waitangi 1984 - Gil Hanly

Hīkoi ki Waitangi 1984 - Gil Hanly

Whina Cooper at Waitangi 1985 - Gil Hanly

Hīkoi ki Waitangi 1984 - Gil Hanly

Hīkoi ki Waitangi 1984 - Gil Hanly

Hīkoi ki Waitangi 1984 - Gil Hanly

Women's workshop at Waitangi 1985 - Gil Hanly

Hīkoi ki Waitangi 1984 - Gil Hanly

Confrontation at Waitangi 1983 - Gil Hanly

Protest at Waitangi - Gil Hanly

Protest at Waitangi 2002 - John Miller

The Land March, the Hīkoi ki Waitangi, and now Hīkoi 2004 have all been large but temperate reminders that the fundamental tenet of staying true to the treaty is shared across the continuum of Māori politics.

Protestors at Waitangi 2002 - John Miller

Chapter Ten
One Billion Pieces of Silver

IN 1990 THE ART EXHIBITION *MANA TIRITI* WAS HELD, FIRST in Wellington and later in Auckland. On reflection the exhibition, which was subtitled *'the art of protest and partnership'*, was a statement in microcosm of the treaty relationship in its sesquicentennial year. It showed the multifarious nature of the Māori protest voice, sitting alongside a revival in traditional Māori art forms such as tā moko and intersecting with politics and history. The exhibition reiterated the importance of understanding contemporary concerns in their historical context, the primacy of the Treaty of Waitangi, and that historical grievances were often hapū and iwi-specific. Delivering strong protest messages, *Mana Tiriti* was guided by the principles of partnership prevalent in public policy at the time. Works were commissioned from Māori and Pākehā artists, and three groups ran the exhibition: the Wellington-based Māori women's art collective Haeata; Project Waitangi, a national provider of treaty education for Pākehā; and the Wellington City Art Gallery. *Mana Tiriti* illustrated the constancy of the protest voice even during the times that considerable rapport was evident in Māori–Pākehā and Māori–Crown relations. [21]

The 1990s looked set to be a period of good news for modern Māori. Hard-won gains from the recent past seemed to be bearing fruit. Iwi-based initiatives and partnerships with government agencies, Māori education, Māori health and social services, Māori media, arts and culture all engaged in the Māori development agenda, transforming the margins of society into a reinvigorated Māori world. There were some improvements; more Māori than before received tertiary education and fewer left school with no qualifications. But urbanisation, economic reform and unemployment still dealt Māori a nasty blow: no improvements repaired the social and economic disparities between Māori and Pākehā, which still remain. In some areas, widespread development activity was supplemented by the settlement of treaty claims, a situation often interpreted as satisfying most Māori and used to account for

Protest against fiscal envelope, Tauranga 1995 - *Bay of Plenty Times*

the quiet on the protest front. It is difficult to say if treaty settlements have satisfied Māori – probably no settlement has been free from opposition – or if they are merely regarded as the best available offer in the prevailing circumstances. Perhaps some of the perceived quietness of the nineties can be attributed to battle-weary iwi recovering from the long and arduous process. Or perhaps interpretations are blurred because too often Māori activism is allowed to be measured by media coverage and the public pronouncements of disgruntled politicians: if it does not exist in headlines, then it does not exist.

Whatever the volume of the protest voice, and whatever the state of the Māori–Crown relationship – good, bad or indifferent – on any given day, the idea that the relationship is given by the Treaty of Waitangi persists. Nothing absolves either party from its treaty obligations. It ought to have come as no surprise to Jim Bolger's National Government, then, that Māori everywhere would have something to say about its 1994 proposal to settle all historical treaty claims within a predetermined 'fiscal envelope' of one billion dollars. It was a proposal prepared with insufficient input from Māori, and presented as an ultimatum rather than a negotiable idea. Māori reaction was swift and wide. Te Kawau Maro, an Auckland-based activist group of Māori tertiary students, demonstrated outside the High Court. Protestors staged a symbolic burning of the formal policy document *'Crown Proposals for the Settlement of Treaty Claims'* on the steps of Parliament at its launch.

Further angry rejection of the proposal was yet to come, and the fact that Sir Hepi Te Heuheu and Dame Te Atairangikaahu declined their invitations to the launch ought to have signalled that many Māori would share the protestors' sentiments. In January 1995, Sir Hepi convened the Hīrangi Hui at Tūrangi to discuss the proposals. Neither a march nor a hīkoi, the Hīrangi Hui did share at least one characteristic with the stands taken in 1975 and 1984: it displayed Māori unity. One thousand tribal representatives – activists, iwi leaders, academics, clerics – came together in opposition to the fiscal envelope. Not only was it inconsistent with the Treaty of Waitangi, but it was also inconsistent with the universal principles of honour and good faith; principles under which settlements were expected to be negotiated. Just as worrying as the fiscal envelope itself, was the fact the some government ministers saw it as a proposal with integrity. The resounding rejection of the fiscal envelope by the Hīrangi Hui was followed by heated Waitangi Day protests. Spit was spat, buttocks bared, a flag trampled and the programme for Waitangi evening cancelled. Jim Bolger responded by threatening an end to Waitangi Day and a possible return to New Zealand Day. It did not happen, but the Government remained aloof from Waitangi for the next three years.

The extent and intensity of Māori disapproval of the fiscal envelope did nothing to deter the Government which continued with its round of thirteen consultation hui. For the Crown at least, thirteen became twelve when the hui set for Mangamuka resolved to tell the Crown it would not be welcomed. The Crown faced protest at every hui it attended.[22] At Tauranga the proposal document was stomped on, at Te Kuiti it was torn to shreds. At Ōpōtiki Tame Iti addressed the Crown from atop a stepladder so that he could look down on them. He also presented Minister of Justice Doug Graham with a submission written on a horse blanket, explaining that he was returning the gift of previous governments with 'the pain of Tūhoe' written on it. But the most unsettling protest action for the then Chief Executive of Te Puni Kōkiri, Wira Gardiner, occurred at Owae Marae in Waitara. A group of about 300 mainly young protestors sat motionless and impassive on the ground, wrapped in grey blankets. There was no heckling, no yelling, no chanting as the Crown contingent passed onto the marae – just silent disapproval. At the same hui, a New Zealand flag was burned, underlining the strength of opposition.

No doubt history will one day give more detailed explanations of the Crown's motivations. But for now it seems that the Crown either misread the strength of Māori concerns, or understood them and chose to ignore them. In the undercurrent of opposition to the fiscal envelope churned a number of other burning issues. There was a general frustration with the time, money and energy-consuming treaty claims and settlements processes. There was also resentment about Māori people's disproportionate representation amongst the casualties of economic reform and long-term unemployment. Throughout the country, these issues were expressed in terms of a Māori desire to control Māori futures and Māori resources: tino rangatiratanga, Māori sovereignty, autonomy, independence, self-determination, mana Māori motuhake. A genuine commitment to a constitutional review, undertaken by Māori and the Crown together, was also called for and was regarded as a means of making a genuine break from the processes of colonial law.

Other actions augmented protests aimed at the fiscal envelope directly, and rested heavily on the foundation stone of Māori activism, tino rangatiratanga. In October 1994, before the policy was officially launched but after it had been announced, Mike Smith chainsawed the lone pine on One Tree Hill on the anniversary of the signing of the 1835 Declaration of Independence. Like Benjamin Nathan's attack on the America's Cup in 1997, it was an act that enraged Pākehā. But it was also an attack on one of the symbols of colonisation and a rejection of the colonial practice of supplanting Māori rights, reminiscent of Hone Heke's felling of the flagstaff at Kororāreka in 1844 in his own political protest against his colonisers. A similar protest occurred in December 1995 when a statue of the nineteenth-century politician, Sir John Ballance, was decapitated. That act foreshadowed a major occupation that would soon commence at Pākaitore in Whanganui.

City Gallery, Wellington

Artwork: *150 years of Dirty Laundry (1990)*.
Artist: Irihapeti Ramsden and Paparangi Reid.

City Gallery, Wellington

Artwork: *Raupatu; Te Kaea; The Waiohau Fraud (1990)*, installation in progress.
Artist: Robert Pouwhare.

In 1990, the art exhibition *Mana Tiriti*
- the art of protest and partnership was held in
Wellington then Auckland to celebrate 150 years
since the signing of the Treaty of Waitangi.

Mahuta Family

O'Regan Family

Office of Treaty Settlements

The 1984 Labour Government extended the role of the Waitangi Tribunal to inquire into historical grievances dating back to 1840. By the 1990s the tribunal had reported to the government on several large claims and recommended generous and long-lasting settlements. Some iwi such as Ngāi Tahu, Tainui and Ngāti Awa reached agreements with the Crown. In 1990 agreement was reached between the Crown and iwi to settle long standing disputes over sea fisheries.

Dominion Post

Protest against fiscal envelope, Wellington 1995 - *Dominion Post Collection, Alexander Turnbull Library*

March protesting against fiscal envelope, Rotorua 1995 - *Fotopress*

Police stamping out burning effigy -
protest against fiscal envelope, Wellington 1995
Dominion Post Collection, Alexander Turnbull Library

Protests against the
'fiscal envelope' occurred
throughout the country.

Flag burning - protest against fiscal envelope, Waitara 1995 - *Daily News*

Chapter Eleven
He Whenua Māori a Pākaitore

Our people are tired, they're fed up, ... having to come and spend over a hundred years trying to say 'This is us, this is what we're trying to hold onto, this is what we have for our future generations'.

(Archie Taiaroa, addressing the Waitangi Tribunal, 1994)

THE EIGHTY-DAY OCCUPATION OF PĀKAITORE IN 1995 WAS THE largest of several that occurred throughout the country during the middle of the 1990s. Tāmaki Girls College, Takahue School, Whakarewarewa, Waikato University and Huntly all became sites of similar active resistance. In Taranaki and Tūhoe sales of lands that had been confiscated in the nineteenth century were disrupted. Deep frustration and impatience underscored the individual history of each grievance. Amongst the leadership at Pākaitore were Ken Mair (who also headed the Māori rights group Te Ahi Kaa), Niko Tangaroa and Tariana Turia. The events that unfolded at Pākaitore were preceded by a couple of curtain-raisers, including the decapitation of the Ballance statue already mentioned. In January, Ken Mair led a brief but effective sit-in at Television New Zealand just as the evening news was about to go to air, to highlight the lack of Māori programming. Then three days before Waitangi Day, Whanganui traffic was disrupted by a road block north of the city. Another Te Ahi Kaa action, it aimed to challenge people to think about the meaning of the day off they were soon to enjoy, and emphasise the historical grievances of Whanganui iwi. The occupation began soon afterwards at the end of February with the establishment of the Pākaitore Marae and a celebration of Whanganuitanga.[23]

At the heart of the Pākaitore story was an historical dispute surrounding the ownership of the area that the city of Whanganui had come to know as Moutoa Gardens. Pākaitore had been one of numerous riverside settlements of Te Āti Haunui-a-Paparangi. Mostly used on a seasonal basis, its occupation by the iwi had continued unchallenged even after 1900. It had been the site of an agreement to sell land at Whanganui, but Māori insisted the site itself had been explicitly excluded from the sale and had long disputed its ownership. In fact, Pākaitore was but one instance of the systematic alienation of land and river from Whanganui iwi. The occupation returned land to its centripetal position in iwi identity, and reclaimed the name and former tikanga of Pākaitore. When claims of sovereignty were later made over a

March in support of Pākaitore occupation, Whanganui 1995 - Leigh Mitchell-Anyon

At the heart of the 80 day occupation of Pākaitore was an historical dispute surrounding the ownership of the area Whanganui City has come to know as Moutoa Gardens.

wider district, it also became a localised statement of the broader issue of self-determination.

In the background to the Pākaitore occupation was the extraordinary denunciation of the Crown's fiscal envelope. Also, Te Āti Haunui-a-Paparangi was at the time part way through the protracted claims process. Lodged in 1990, their claim asserted that Te Āti Haunui-a-Paparangi had never ceded its ownership of the river to anybody, let alone the Crown. The Waitangi Tribunal heard the details of the claim between March and July 1994, and reported in 1999.[24] Like Bastion Point almost twenty years before, the claim was an example of the layering of grievance upon grievance. The history of petitioning for the Crown's consideration was more than one hundred years old, and the desire for resolution became more urgent as iwi were effectively excluded from modern management of the river. Since 1960 the headwaters of the Whanganui River had been diverted to generate electricity, and forty years of formal objections to the absence of consultation with iwi were ignored. In 2003, after the tribunal reported and after Pākaitore was resolved, Whanganui iwi still found themselves making a stand for their river – opposing a resource consent to continue diverting the headwaters for another thirty-five years. Iwi rights were being stripped away before they were even restored; and drawn out legal proceedings tested both patience and limited resources.

Pākehā were losing patience too. It looked like protest begat protest, and the Government was called on to take a bolder stand. At Whanganui, as the occupants settled in, a pou erected by the nineteenth-century military leader Major Te Rangihiwinui Te Keepa was cut down, and the One New Zealand Foundation demonstrated outside Pākaitore. An Anzac Day procession protested by marching past the gardens, and was followed by the establishment of the group 'One Wanganui' which refuted the relevance of the treaty in modern New Zealand. Predictably, church leaders appealed for understanding and reasoned debate.

The mayor, Chas Poynter, wanted the situation to be resolved from within the Whanganui community. He attempted to negotiate a solution that would re-site offensive monuments, put the land in a trust, and see that its ownership and that of other disputed sites was researched. Poynter was unwilling to negotiate with the protestors while they occupied Pākaitore, and no firm response to his proposed solution was forthcoming. By the end of March, the number of people at Pākaitore had increased from about 150 to more than 400. The Whanganui District Council went to the High Court to have ownership of the gardens clarified. The court, which was spurned by the protestors, ruled in the council's favour. An eviction notice was served, and on 18 May 1995 the occupants peacefully left the gardens.

What happened at Pākaitore in 1995 shared many of the characteristics of the land-rights movement of the 1970s. People were reminded of the occupation of Bastion Point, a repetition of history that many would have preferred to avoid. Pākaitore illustrated how unresolved long-standing grievances get interlaced with contemporary concerns and feed discontent. It encapsulated the perpetual fundamentals of Māori protest – land and the treaty – and was a site-specific expression of the wider kaupapa of rangatiratanga. In the years since 1995, Whanganui iwi have returned to commemorate the event. In 1999 the Waitangi Tribunal's report upheld the claims of Te Āti Haunui-a-Paparangi. The report reiterated the rangatiratanga of Āti Haunui over the river and its tributaries. It also urged that the Crown recognise Āti Haunui authority, and ensure contemporary management of the river proceed collaboratively. In 2001 Pākaitore was vested as a historic reserve. Owned by the Crown, it is now administered by a board consisting of iwi, council and Crown representatives.

March against fiscal envelope and in support of Pākaitore occupation, Whanganui 1995 - Leigh Mitchell-Anyon

Leigh Mitchell-Anyon

Pākaitore illustrated how unresolved long-standing grievances get interlaced with contemporary concerns and feed discontent.

Leigh Mitchell-Anyon

Leigh Mitchell-Anyon

Debating the issues in Whanganui 1995 - Leigh Mitchell-Anyon

March in support of Pākaitore occupation, Whanganui 1995 - Leigh Mitchell-Anyon

The mayor, Chas Poynter, wanted the situation to be resolved from within the Whanganui community. In 1999 the Waitangi Tribunal upheld the claims of Te Āti Haunui-a-Paparangi. In 2001 Pākaitore was vested as a historic reserve. Owned by the Crown, it is now administered by a board consisting of iwi, council and Crown representatives.

Mayor of Whanganui visits Pākaitore 1995 - Leigh Mitchell-Anyon

Chapter Twelve

Ake, Ake, Ake

THE GOALS OF MĀORI DEVELOPMENT – the pursuit and reinvigoration of tino rangatiratanga, now generations old – are shared by Māori whether they are activists or not, and are apparent in the things that are a cause for celebration and the things that cause conflict and tension. In the modern era Māori innovation has blossomed, its fruits broadcast daily on Māori radio and television, and seen in the pages of Māori magazines and newspapers. And protest and activism remains; often misrepresented and misunderstood by its detractors, it now seems part of the nation's cultural character. Waitangi Day protests, occupations, demonstrations and hikoi have continued into the new millennium alongside submissions, litigation, claims and settlements.

In 2002 two occupations caught the media's attention – one at Ngāwhā in the North, the other at Te Kurī a Paoa (Young Nick's Head) on the East Coast. At Ngāwhā, protestors occupied the site at which a new prison was to be built, after a year of unsatisfactory progress opposing construction of the prison through formal channels. The issue at Te Kurī a Paoa was its proposed sale to an overseas interest. Though both protests were triggered by contemporary events, they were also inseparable from their iwi pasts.

Ngāwhā is known for its geothermal springs, highly valued taonga central to the hapū and iwi narratives of the area. Even if the politics of prisons and imprisonment could be set aside, the building would disrupt the mauri of the springs, and therefore the ancestral relationships implicit in its location within tribal lore. The site included an eighteenth-century battle ground, wāhi tapu, and the lair of the taniwha Takauere, the protection of which had been considered by the Waitangi Tribunal in 1993.

Similarly, Te Kurī a Paoa was imbued with Ngāi Tāmanuhiri history and identity. Besides being the identifying maunga of the iwi, it was the site where Paoa, the

Protest at Te Kuri a Paoa (Young Nick's Head) 2002 - *Gisborne Herald*

captain of the waka *Horouta*, first landed and contained a 600-year-old settlement with fifteen archaeological sites. Te Kurī a Paoa also touched Pākehā history, when it was sighted by Captain Cook in 1769.

The activists at both Ngāwhā and Te Kurī a Paoa had traversed the official avenues available to them before beginning their protests. At Ngāwhā, before any attempt was made to occupy the prison site, well over a year was spent in legal proceedings in an attempt to stop the required resource consent, which the Northland Regional Council had initially refused. Similarly, Ngāi Tāmanuhiri spent months in the submissions process of the Overseas Investment Commission before resorting to the occupation of Te Kurī a Paoa. Both Ngāwhā and Te Kurī a Paoa were examples of local site-specific land protests, redolent of the land rights movement of the 1970s. Yet they were each also spurred by twenty-first century concerns. Prison building, the efficacy of the justice system, and the selling off of Aotearoa are modern issues debated amongst the wider community, and not just Māori or Māori and the Crown.

Ngāi Tāmanuhiri eventually arrived at a reasonable resolution and met with the new owner almost a year after the sale had first been proposed. Te Kurī a Paoa was vested as an historic reserve, public access to it retained, and use and development of the area restricted by covenant. Resolving Ngāwhā was less satisfactory: construction of the new correctional facility did not subdue opposition to it. The prison was one of many issues canvassed in the lead up to Waitangi Day celebrations in 2003. The issue was raised again in September that year, during discussions that eventually led to the cancellation of the Government's proposed foreshore and seabed consultation hui at Whāngārei. Land and the treaty – familiar threads of Māori protest – have continued to interweave with a broader movement aimed at contesting government attempts to appropriate Māori rights. Just how broad that movement is was clearly demonstrated on 5 May 2004, when Hīkoi 2004 arrived at Parliament.

It is no surprise that the pattern of reasoned engagement with the issues using official channels preceded the Hīkoi. The beginnings of the foreshore and seabed story may be found in the Marlborough Sounds. Concerned about the way marine farming was developing in the sounds, Te Tau Ihu o Te Waka a Māui, representing iwi at the top of the South Island, laid a claim with the Waitangi Tribunal in 1996. In 1997, the same iwi applied to the Māori Land Court to have its customary ownership of the takutaimoana determined. Widely regarded as a test case, the Māori Land Court had in fact investigated title to lakebeds, and the foreshore and seabed before. The Crown appealed, and in 2002 the High Court decided that New Zealand law prevented Māori from taking their claims to the takutaimoana to the Māori Land Court. On 19 July 2003, however, the Court of Appeal determined the opposite, that the Māori Land Court indeed had jurisdiction to investigate Māori customary ownership of the foreshore and seabed. Within days the Government announced

Protest sign at Ngāwhā 2002 - *Northern Advocate*

In 2002, two occupations caught the media's attention – one at Ngāwhā in the North, the other at Te Kura a Paoa (Young Nick's Head) on the East Coast. At Ngāwhā, protestors occupied the site at which a new prison was built. The issue at Te Kuri a Paoa was the proposed sale to an overseas buyer.

Gisborne Herald

March in support of Te Kuri a Paoa (Young Nick's Head) 2002 - *Gisborne Herald*

March against prison at Ngāwhā 2002 - *Northern Advocate*

that it would assert Crown ownership of the country's foreshore and seabed, and enact legislation to disallow Māori claims of customary ownership. The Government response flabbergasted many people, not just Māori. Its swift reaction seemed ill-conceived, heavy-handed and premature.

Fervent debate followed, and the Pandora's Box that is New Zealand's race relations was opened on the nation's beaches, holding the gaze of media headlines that tried to unravel the myths of national identity and One-New-Zealandism by asking questions like 'What's Eating Pākehā?' and 'Who Are You?'.[25] Labour's Māori ministers of Parliament formally warned their government to consult Māori and seek their cooperation before extinguishing their customary rights so arbitrarily. Thousands of iwi representatives met at hui around the country to organise and convey their opposition to the Government's position. Five hundred Pākehā protested in Nelson asserting Pākehā rights, and ninety protestors rallied on Takapuna Beach declaring the beaches sacrosanct to all New Zealanders. The National Party embarked on a 'Beaches For All' campaign and attracted 40,000 signatures to its online petition calling for the Government to claim exclusive Crown ownership of the foreshore and seabed.

Labour launched a discussion document and dedicated much of September to a round of consultation hui. Not surprisingly, protest featured at several of the hui, one of the most memorable occurring at Mataiwhetu Marae near Thames. There, kaumātua Toko Renata, chairperson of the Hauraki Maori Trust Board, returned his Queen's Service Medal and New Zealand Merit Award to the Deputy Prime Minister Michael Cullen. Overall, the hui resoundingly rejected and condemned Labour's proposals, repeating a pattern seen less than ten years earlier when the National government had promulgated its fiscal envelope. The Government analysed more than 2,000 public submissions and released its foreshore and seabed plan a week before Christmas Day, advocating that title be held in perpetuity by the people of New Zealand. Many Māori spent much of their summer preparing submissions and giving evidence to the Waitangi Tribunal, their only distraction being Don Brash's speech made to an audience happily ensconced at Orewa-by-the-Sea. Waitangi Day 2004, which included mud-slinging of the literal kind – directed at Brash – served as another reminder of Māori dissatisfaction with the Government's approach.

The day after Waitangi Day, Te Rarawa hosted Hands Across the Beach at the southern end of Te Oneroa a Tohe. Under the slogan 'Tiakina te Takutaimoana' a pouwhenua commemorating the Te Rarawa tupuna Poroa was unveiled at dawn at a place called Paripari. Then a day of speech-making, entertainment and games followed. The whole event concluded with a line of thousands of people stretched for two kilometres down the foreshore, united in their acknowledgement of the roles

John Miller

Gil Hanly

Gil Hanly

Te Rarawa hosted the Hands Across the Beach event at the southern end of Te Oneroa a Tohe (90 Mile Beach) which concluded with a line of thousands of New Zealanders stretched for two kilometres along the foreshore, united in their acknowledgement of the relationship of local iwi with the takutaimoana.

John Miller

Gil Hanly

Hīkoi 2004 became a spectacular display of Māori transcending tribal difference to express their shared dissatisfaction with government policy. Conservative and radical alike joined the Hīkoi along its route to Wellington and witnessed the unifying effect of shared issues as the footfalls of Māori activism continue to imprint society and politics -
ake, ake, ake.

Gil Hanly

Gil Hanly

Gil Hanly

Gil Hanly

Gil Hanly

John Miller

Gil Hanly

Gil Hanly

Gil Hanly

and relationships of local iwi with the takutaimoana. Participants described the day as magic, mind-blowing and moving. The media seemed to enjoy the event also. Much fun must have been had preparing the 'good Māori, bad Māori' show for the evening news which presented the demonstration at Te Oneroa a Tohe as serene next to the previous day's mud-slinging and conflict. In fact, many people attended both days' events, including a number of overseas visitors.

The year 2004 marched on, and Māori conservative and radical alike marched also. The Hīkoi reached Parliament in time to hear Labour's proposed Foreshore and Seabed Bill pass its first reading. Tariana Turia left the Labour Party over the issue, and forced a by-

election in Te Taihauauru which she won easily. It was a good omen for the Māori Party, the new political force for Māori that has harnessed the energy and leadership that made the Hīkoi such a success. It is easy for detractors to dismiss its viability, especially when the value and relevance of Māori activism are measured by media headlines and politicians' one-liners. But throughout history and all about the Māori nation there are reminders of the importance and achievements of those at the forefront of Māori protest, bearing the flag of tino rangatiratanga. As the takutaimoana issue continues to be played out, history once again witnesses the unifying effect of land loss, and the footfalls of Māori activism continue to imprint society and politics – ake, ake, ake.

Hīkoi at Parliament 2004 - Clayton Tume

Footnotes

1. Aroha Harris, 'Maori and the "Maori Affairs"', in Dalley, Bronwyn & Margaret Tennant, eds, *Past Judgement: History and Social Policy,* Dunedin, 2004.

2. See for example, R. H. T. Thompson, 'Maori Affairs and the New Zealand Press', *Journal of the Polynesian Society (JPS),* 64, 1, 1955, and 'European Attitudes to Maoris: a projective approach', *JPS,* 68, 3, 1959; and Dane & Mary Archer, 'Race, Identity and the Maori People', *JPS,* 79, 2, 1970.

3. See John Harre, 'A Case of Racial Discrimination in New Zealand', 71, 2, 1962.

4. Ans Westra, *Washday At the Pa,* revised edition, Christchurch, 1964; and Caxton Press, *Washday At the Pa:* Publisher's Note, Christchurch, 1964.

5. Useful summaries and brief analyses of legislation affecting Maori and Maori land are given by David Williams, The Maori Land Legislation Database, (available at: http://www.library.auckland.ac.nz/).

6. Petition of Bishop of Aotearoa W. N. Panapa and others, circa. 1961, MA 1, 36/1/21 vol 2, Archives New Zealand, Wellington.

7. 'Remits - 1969 conference', MA 1, 36/26/11 part 3, Archives New Zealand, Wellington.

8. Ranginui Walker discusses the advent of Nga Tamatoa subsequent to this conference in *Ka Whawhai Tonu Matou,* Auckland, 1990, pp.208-212, and 'The Genesis of Maori Activism', *JPS,* 93, 3, 1984.

9. Waitangi Tribunal, *Te Reo Maori Claim (Wai 11),* Wellington, 1989.

10. Michael King, *Being Pakeha Now: reflections and recollections of a white native,* Auckland, 1999, p. 105.

11. News Bulletin, Te Matakite o Aotearoa, May 1976, 'Matakite and the Maori Land March, 1979', papers compiled by Ranginui Walker, University of Auckland, Auckland.

12. Negotiations- Re Raglan Golf Course, and Newsletter Two, 'Matakite and the Maori Land March, 1979', papers compiled by Ranginui Walker, University of Auckland, Auckland.

13. *Mana* Magazine, 20, 1998, pp.6-9.

14. Michael King discusses the Land March in relation to Whina's involvement in chapter eleven of *Whina,* Auckland, 1983. Refer also to the Vivian Hutchinson Collection, Manuscripts and Archives, Alexander Turnbull Library, Wellington.

15. A cogent history of Ngāti Whātua of Ōrākei may be found in the Waitangi Tribunal's report, *Report of the Waitangi Tribunal on the Orakei Claim* (Wai 9), Wellington, 1987.

16. The occupation is detailed in Sharon Hawke, *Takaparawha: the people's story: Bastion Point 20 year commemoration book,* Auckland, 1998; and Walker, *Ka Whawhai Tonu Matou,* pp. 215-219.

17. Discussion about major developments in Maori policy and Maori politics during this period may be found in: Mason Durie, *Te Mana, Te Kawanatanga: the politics of Maori self-determination,* Auckland, 1998; G. V. Butterworth & H. R. Young, *Maori Affairs: Nga Take,* Wellington, 1990, chapter nine; and Walker, *Ka Whawhai Tonu Matou,* chapters eleven and twelve.

18. Walker discusses both these events in *Ka Whawhai Tonu Matou,* pp. 220-7. Additional information is available from 'He Taua and the Haka Party, 1979', and 'Race Relations, 1970-1983', papers compiled by Ranginui Walker, University of Auckland, Auckland.

19. Ranginui Walker, *Ka Whawhai Tonu Matou,* p. 220.

20. Walker considers Waitangi Day and related activism in chapter eleven of *Ka Whawhai Tonu Matou.* He has also collated newspaper cuttings and newsletters in 'Treaty of Waitangi, celebrations, 1983-1989', 'Waitangi Action Committee, 1981-83', University of Auckland, Auckland.

21. Young, Ramari, ed., *Mana Tiriti: the art of protest and partnership,* Wellington, 1991.

22. Events at the fiscal envelope hui are detailed in: Wira Gardiner, *Return to Sender: what really happened at the fiscal envelope hui,* Auckland, 1996.

23. The occupation that unfolded at Pākaitore is outlined in. Durie, *Te Mana, Te Kawanatanga,* pp. 125-9.

24. Waitangi Tribunal, *The Whanganui River Report (Wai 167),* Wellington, 1999.

25. New Zealand Herald, 21 February 2004, and Bruce Ansley, 'Who are you?', *New Zealand Listener,* 190, 3305, September 2003.

Glossary

ake, ake, ake	forever and ever
arohanui	great affectionate regard
hapū	subtribe
He whenua Māori a Pākaitore	Pākaitore is Māori land
iwi	tribe
kaitiaki	guardian
karakia	incantation, prayer
kaumātua	elders
kaupapa	plan, scheme, proposal
ka whawhai tonu mātou	we continue to fight
Kīngitanga	the king movement
Ko te reo te mauri o te mana Māori	the language is the life force of mana Māori
kōhanga reo	Māori-medium preschool
kōkiri	advance
kōkiri centre	community-led training centre
kuia	elderly woman
mana	power, authority, prestige; psychic force
Mana Māori Motuhake	separate Māori mana
Mana Tiriti	the mana of the Treaty of Waitangi
manawhenua	authority or control over land
manuhiri	visitor
marae	a ceremonial courtyard; a complex of land and buildings associated with such a courtyard
maranga mai	rise up
maunga	mountain
mauri	life force or life essence
pā	a fortified place, a small Māori community
papakāinga	home, residence, village settlement
pouwhenua	a symbolic pole or post expressing manawhenua
pupuri whenua	keep the land
rangatahi	youth
rangatiratanga	sovereignty, leadership, chieftainship, self-management
raupatu	land confiscation
takutaimoana	foreshore and seabed
tangata whenua	local people, people of the land
taniwha	water monster, environmental gaurdian
taonga	a treasured or valued thing
te reo	the language; the Māori language
te reo me ōna tikanga	the language and its protocol
tino rangatiratanga	Māori control of Māori resources
tū tangata	stand tall
tupuna	ancestor, grandparent
tūrangawaewae	home, a place for the feet
urupā	cemetery
wāhi tapu	sacred sites
whakapohane	expose the buttocks (as an insult)
whakatauākī	proverb
whānau	family, extended family
whanaunga	relation
Whanganuitanga	matters pertaining to the Whanganui River and its people

Bibliography

A Note on Sources

Ranginui Walker's *Ka Whawhai Tonu Mātou*, that intrepid milestone in Aotearoa New Zealand history, was an immediate and invaluable source from the time work on this book began. Walker has also gifted a remarkable collection of unpublished papers, press clippings and ephemera covering all aspects of Māori life and politics to the University of Auckland library. That collection and numerous of Walker's publications, listed below, were the staple sources on which this book relied, and underline the indispensability of his endeavours to this project.

Amongst the other sources, some were relied upon more than others according to their relevance to particular chapters. They include: the newsletters *Te Hokioi* and *MOOHR*; pertinent Waitangi Tribunal reports; Sharon Hawke's *Takaparawha*; Te Kawariki's *Twenty Years of Protest Action, 1979-1999*; Michael King's *Whina*; and Wira Gardiner's *Return to Sender*. Walker's *Ka Whawhai Tonu Matou*, Mason Durie's *Te Mana, Te Kawanatanga*, Graeme Butterworth and Hepora Young's *Maori Affairs*, and Erik Schwimmer's *Maori People in the Nineteen-Sixties*, all usefully provided general understandings of Maori policy and political development. James Belich's *Paradise Reforged*, Michael King's *Penguin History of New Zealand*, the *Dictionary of New Zealand Biography*, and the websites of relevant iwi and other organisations were all variously consulted for background and general information. These and other readings were supplemented by newspaper, archive and manuscript research.

Useful Websites

http://www.dnzb.govt.nz/dnzb/
http://www.terarawa.co.nz/
http://www.tetaurawhiri.govt.nz/
http://www.teope.co.nz/ (Te Ope Mana a Tai)
http://www.wrmtb.co.nz/ (Wanganui River aori Trust Board)
http://www.treatyofwaitangi.govt.nz
http://www.waitangi-tribunal.govt.nz/
http://www.nzhistory.net.nz/
http://aotearoa.wellington.net.nz/

Newspapers and Periodicals

Auckland Star   *Dominion Post*
Mana   *New Zealand Listener*
Northern Advocate   *Sunday Star Times*
New Zealand Herald   *Bay of Plenty Times*
Daily News   *Gisborne Herald*
Fotopress   *Tū Mai*

Photographic Collections

John Miller, private collection.   Leigh Mitchell-Anyon, private collection.
Gil Hanly, private collection.   O'Regan Family, private collection.
Clayton Tume, private collection.   Mahuta Family, private collection.
Auckland Art Gallery Toi o Tamaki.   City Gallery Wellington.
Māori Television Service.   Office of Treaty Settlements
Photographic Archive, Alexander Turnbull Library, Wellington.
Archives New Zealand/Te Rua Mahara o te Kāwanatanga.
Christian Heinegg collection, Alexander Turnbull Library, Wellington.
Ans Westra collection, Alexander Turnbull Library, Wellington.

Archives and Manuscripts

Printed Ephemera Collection, Alexander Turnbull Library, Wellington.
New Zealand Cartoon Archive, Alexander Turnbull Library, Wellington.
Vivian Hutchinson (Papers Relating to Te Matakite o Aotearoa)
Collection, Manuscripts and Archives, Alexander Turnbull Library.
Māori Affairs (Head Office) Series, Archives New Zealand, Wellington.
—— (Whangarei) Series, Archives New Zealand, Auckland.
—— (Auckland) Series, Archives New Zealand, Auckland.
Papers compiled by Ranginui Walker, University of Auckland Library, Auckland.

Library

Te Hokioi, (vol. 1, issues 1-6), compiled 1979.
Māori Organisation on Human Rights, 1980.
Ngā Tamatoa, 1980
Race relations, 1970–1983.
Race relations, 1984–1989, file 2
Matakite and the Māori land march, 1979.
He Taua and the haka party, 1979.
Treaty of Waitangi, celebrations, 1983–1989.

Waitangi Action Committee, 1981–1983.
Mana Motuhake, 1980.
Mana Motuhake, 1980–1988, file 2, 1988.
Māori Affairs, 1980–1989.
Bastion Point, 1979.
Māori Land, 1980–1988: Bastion Point 1981–1988, file 2.
Motunui outfall and Waitangi Day protests, 1983.

Radio Programmes

Paul Diamond, (producer), 'Ngā Tamatoa: The Māori protest group Ngā Tamatoa thirty years on', Radio New Zealand, 2001.

Books, Articles and Theses

Archer, Dane & Mary, 'Race, Identity and the Maori People', *Journal of the Polynesian Society*, 79, 2, 1970.

Archie, Carol, *Maori Sovereignty: the Pakeha perspective*, Auckland, 1995.

Ausubel, D. B., *The Fern and the Tiki: an American view of New Zealand national character, social attitudes, and race relations*, New York, 1965.

Awatere, Donna, *Maori Sovereignty*, Auckland, 1984.

Awatere, Donna, *My Journey*, Auckland, 1996.

Ballara, Angela, *Proud to be White? A survey of Pakeha prejudice in New Zealand*, Auckland, 1986.

Belich, James, *Paradise Reforged: a history of the New Zealanders from the 1880s to the year 2000*, Auckland, 2001.

——, *Making Peoples: a history of the New Zealanders from Polynesian settlement to the end of the nineteenth century*, Auckland, 1996.

Bell, Claudia, *Inventing New Zealand: everyday myths of Pakeha identity*, Auckland, 1996.

Binney, Judith, 'The Treaty of Waitangi', in *Towards 1990*, Atholl Anderson et. al. (eds), Wellington, 1990.

Brash, Don, 'Nationhood', address to the Orewa Rotary Club, 27 January 2004.

Brown, Amy, *Mana Wahine: women who show the way*, Auckland, 1994.

Butterworth, G. V. & H. R. Young, *Maori Affairs Nga Take Maori*, Wellington, 1990.

Byrnes, Giselle, *The Waitangi Tribunal and New Zealand History*, Auckland, 2004.

Caxton Press, *Washday at the Pa: publisher's note*, Christchurch, 1964.

Coates, K. S. & P. G. McHugh, *Living Relationships, Kokiri Ngatahi: the Treaty of Waitangi in the new millennium*, Wellington, 1998.

Consedine, R. & J., *Healing Our History*, Auckland, 2001.

Cox, Lindsay, *Kotahitanga: the search for Maori unity*, Auckland, 1993.

Department of Justice, *Principles for Crown Action on the Treaty of Waitangi*, Wellington, 1989.

Diamond, Paul, *A Fire in your Belly:Māori Leaders Speak*, Wellington 2003

Durie, Mason, *Te Mana, Te Kawanatanga: the politics of Maori self-determination*, Auckland, *1998.*
——, *Whaiora: Maori health development*, Auckland, 1994.

Fisher, Ronald J., *Conflict and Collaboration in Maori–Pakeha Relations*, Hamilton, 1984.

Fleras, Augie & Paul Spoonley, *Recalling Aotearoa: indigenous politics and ethnic relations in New Zealand*, Auckland, 1999.

Fox, Derek T., 'The Mass Media: a Maori perspective', *Report of the Royal Commission on Social Policy*, Wellington, 1988.

Gardiner, Wira, *Return to Sender: what really happened at the fiscal envelope hui,* Auckland, 1996.

Graham, D., *Trick or Treaty?,* Wellington, 1997.

Greenland, Hauraki, 'Ethnicity as Ideology: the critique of Pakeha society' in *Tauiwi: racism and ethnicity in New Zealand,* P. Spoonley et al. (eds), Palmerston North, 1984.

Harris, Aroha, 'Maori Land Development Schemes, 1945–1974, with two case studies from the Hokianga', M.Phil thesis, Massey University, 1996.

——, 'Maori and the "Maori Affairs"', in *Past Judgement: History and Social Policy,* B. Dalley & M. Tennant, eds, Dunedin, 2004.

Harre, John, 'A Case of Racial Discrimination in New Zealand', *Journal of the Polynesian Society,* 71, 2, 1962.

Hawke, Sharon, *Takaparawha: the people's story: 1998 Bastion Point 20 year commemoration book, Moko Productions,* Orakei, 1998.

Hazlehurst, K. M., *Political Expression and Ethnicity: statecraft and mobilisation in the Maori world,* Connecticut, 1993.

——, *Racial Conflict and Resolution in New Zealand: the haka party incident and its aftermath 1979–1980,* Canberra, 1988.

Howe, K., *Race Relations Australia and New Zealand: a comparative survey 1770s–1970s,* Auckland, 1977.

Human Rights Commission, *Racial Harmony in New Zealand: a statement of issues,* Auckland, 1979.

Hunn, J. K., *Report on the Department of Maori Affairs,* Wellington, 1961.

Ihimaera, Witi, ed., *Growing Up Maori,* Auckland, 1998.

——, et al., eds, *Regaining Aotearoa: Maori writers speak out,* Auckland, 1993.

Jones, Lloyd, 'Images of Maori in the Pakeha Press: Pakeha representations of Maori in the popular print media, 1935-1965', MA thesis, University of Auckland, 1998.

Kawharu, I. H., *Maori Land Tenure: studies of a changing institution,* New York, 1977.

——, ed., *Waitangi: Maori and Pakeha perspectives of the Treaty of Waitangi,* Auckland, 1989.

——, ed., *Conflict and Compromise: essays on the Maori since colonisation,* Auckland, 2003.

——, 'Land and Identity in Tamaki: a Ngati Whatua Perspective', Hilary Lecture, Auckland War Memorial Museum, 2001.

Kelsey, J., *A Question of Honour: Labour and the Treaty, 1984–1989,* Wellington, 1990.

Kernot, B., ed., *Te Reo o Te Tiriti Mai Rano: the treaty is always speaking,* Wellington, 1989.

King, Michael, *The Penguin History of New Zealand,* Auckland, 2003.

——, *Being Pakeha Now: reflections and recollections of a white native,* Auckland, 1999.

——, *Being Pakeha,* Auckland, 1988.

——, ed., *Pakeha: the quest for identity in New Zealand,* Auckland, 1991.

——, *Maori: a photographic and social history,* Auckland, 1983.

——, *Whina: a biography of Whina Cooper,* Auckland, 1983.

——, ed., *Tihe Mauri Ora: aspects of Maoritanga,* Auckland, 1978.

——, ed., *Te Ao Hurihuri: the world moves on,* Wellington, 1975.

Laidlaw, Chris, *Rights of Passage: beyond the New Zealand identity crisis,* Auckland, 1999.

Levine, S., & R. Vasil *Maori Political Perspectives: he whakaaro Maori mo nga tikanga kawanatanga,* Auckland, 1985.

Melbourne, Hineani, *Maori Sovereignty: the Maori perspective,* Auckland, 1995.

Metge, Joan, *A New Maori Migration: rural and urban relations in northern New Zealand, Melbourne,* 1964.

——., *The Maoris of New Zealand: Rautahi, 2nd ed.,* London, 1976.

Mihaka, Te Ringa Mangu, *Whakapohane,* Porirua, 1984.

Miller, Harold, *Race Conflict in New Zealand,* Auckland, 1966.

Mol, J. J., 'Race Relations, with Special Reference to New Zealand: a theoretical discussion', *Journal of the Polynesian Society,* 73, 4, 1964.

Novitz, D., & B. Wilmot, eds, *Culture and Identity,* Wellington, 1989.

Office of Treaty Settlements, *Crown Proposals for the Settlement of Treaty of Waitangi Claims,* Wellington, 1995.

Oliver, W. and C. Orange, eds, *Dictionary of New Zealand Biography,* Vols 1, 2, 3, 4 & 5, Wellington, 1990, 1993, 1996, 1998, 2000. (Also available online at: http://www.dnzb.govt.nz/dnzb/.)

Oliver, W. H., *Claims to the Waitangi Tribunal,* Wellington, 1991.

Orange, Claudia, *The Treaty of Waitangi,* Wellington, 1987.

——., 'An Exercise in Maori Autonomy: the rise and fall of the Maori War Effort Organisation', *New Zealand Journal of History,* April, 1987.

Poata-Smith, Evan S. Te Ahu, 'He Pokeke Uenuku I Tu Ai: The Evolution of Contemporary Maori Protest' in *Nga Patai: racism and ethnic relations in Aotearoa/New Zealand,* Paul Spoonley et al., eds, Palmerston North, 1996.

Race Relations Conciliator, *Race Against Time,* Wellington, 1982.

Renwick, W. L., *The Treaty Now,* Wellington, 1990.

Richards, Trevor, *Dancing on Our Bones: South Africa, New Zealand, rugby and racism,* Wellington, 1999.

Schwimmer, Erik, ed., *The Maori People in the Nineteen-Sixties: a symposium,* Auckland, 1968.

Sharp, A., *Justice and the Maori: Maori claims in New Zealand political argument in the 1980s,* Auckland, 1997.

——., 'The Waitangi Tribunal', in *New Zealand Politics in Transition,* R. Miller, ed., Auckland, 1997.

Simpson, Miria, *Nga Tohu o te Tiriti: making a mark,* Wellington, 1990.

Slack, David, *Bullshit, Backlash and Bleeding Hearts: a confused person's guide to the great race row,* Auckland, 2004.

Sorrenson, M. P. K., 'Giving Better Effect to the Treaty', *New Zealand Journal of History,* 2, 24, 1990.

——., 'The Waitangi Tribunal and the Resolution of Maori Grievances', *British Review of New Zealand Studies,* December 1995.

——., *Integration or Identity? Cultural interaction in New Zealand since 1911,* Auckland, 1977.

Spoonley, P. et al., eds, *Tauiwi: racism and ethnicity in New Zealand,* Palmerston North, 1984.

——., et al., eds, *Nga Take: ethnic relations and racism in Aotearoa/New Zealand,* Palmerston North, 1991.

——, *Racism and Ethnicity,* Auckland, 1988.

——, & W. Hirsch, *Between the Lines: racism and the New Zealand media, Auckland,* 1990.

——, D. Pearson, & C. McPherson, eds, *Nga Patai: racism and ethnic relations in Aotearoa/New Zealand,* Palmerston North, 1996.

Tauroa, Hiwi, *Healing the Breach: one Maori's perspective on the Treaty of Waitangi,* Auckland, 1989.

Te Awekotuku, Ngahuia, *Mana Wahine Maori,* Auckland, 1991.

Te Kawariki, *Twenty Years of Protest Action 1979–1999,* Kaitaia, c. 1999.

Temm, P. B., *The Waitangi Tribunal: the conscience of the nation,* Auckland, 1990.

Thompson, R. H. T., 'Maori Affairs and the New Zealand Press', *Journal of the Polynesian Society,* 64, 1, 1955.

——, 'European Attitudes to Maoris: a projective approach', *Journal of the Polynesian Society,* 68, 3, 1959.

Vasil, Raj, *Biculturalism: reconciling Aotearoa with New Zealand,* Wellington, 1988.

Waitangi Tribunal, *Report of the Waitangi Tribunal on the Orakei Claim (Wai 9),* Wellington, 1987.

——, *Report of the Waitangi Tribunal on the Motunui-Waitara Claim (Wai 6),* Wellington, 1989.

——, *Report of the Waitangi Tribunal on a Claim by J. P. Hawke and others of Ngati Whatua Concerning the Fisheries Regulations (Wai 1),* Wellington, 1989.

——, *Report of the Waitangi Tribunal on Claims Concerning the Allocation of Radio Frequencies (Wai 26 and Wai 150),* Wellington, 1990.

——, *The Whanganui River Report (Wai 167),* Wellington, 1999.

——, *The Te Reo Maori Claim (Wai 11),* Wellington, 1989.

Waitangi Tribunal Division, *Te Roopu Whakamana i te Tiriti o Waitangi: a guide to the Waitangi Tribunal,* Wellington, 1993.

Walker, Ranginui, *Ka Whawhai Tonu Matou: struggle without end,* Auckland, 1990.

——, *Nga Pepa a Ranginui: the Walker papers,* Auckland, 1996.

——, The Genesis of Maori Activism', *Journal of the Polynesian Society,* 93, 3, 1984.

——, *Nga Tau Tohetohe: years of anger,* Auckland, 1987.

——, 'The Treaty of Waitangi as the Focus of Maori Protest', in *Waitangi: Maori and Pakeha perspectives of the Treaty of Waitangi,* I. H. Kawharu (ed.), Auckland, 1989.

——, 'Maori People Since 1950', in *The Oxford History of New Zealand, 2nd edn,* Geoffrey W. Rice, ed., Wellington, 1992.

Walsh, D. S., 'Inter-ethnic Relations in New Zealand: a recent controversy', *Journal of the Polynesian Society,* 73, 3, 1964.

Ward, Alan, *Unsettled History: treaty claims in New Zealand today,* Wellington, 1999.

—— 'History and Historians Before the Waitangi Tribunal', *New Zealand Journal of History,* 24, 2, 1990.

Westra, Ans, *Washday at the Pa,* Christchurch, 1964.

Williams, David V., *The Maori Land Legislation Database,* URL: http://www.library.auckland.ac.nz/databases/learn_database/public.asp?record=maoland

Wilson, Margaret & Anna Yeatman, eds, *Justice and Identity: antipodean practices,* Wellington, 1995.

Young, Ramari, ed., *Mana Tiriti: the art of protest and partnership,* Wellington, 1991.